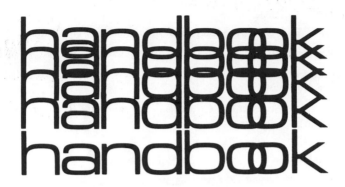

FOR ADMINISTRATORS AND TEACHERS
Reading in the Kindergarten

Edited by Lloyd O. Ollila
University of Victoria
For the Early Childhood and Reading Development Committee

International Reading Association
800 Barksdale Road   Newark, Delaware 19711

INTERNATIONAL READING ASSOCIATION

Copyright 1980 by the
International Reading Association, Inc.

Library of Congress Cataloging in Publication Data
Main entry under title:

Handbook for administrators and teachers.
  Bibliography: p.
  1. Reading (Kindergarten)—Handbooks, manuals,
etc. I. Ollila, Lloyd O.
LB 1181.2.H36   372.4   80-11047
ISBN 0-87207-728-4

Second Printing, September 1982

Contents

Contributors

James Childs
Hopkins Public Schools
Hopkins, Minnesota

John Downing
University of Victoria

Jeanne Hammond
Hopkins Public Schools
Hopkins, Minnesota

Terry Johnson
University of Victoria

Sara Lundsteen
North Texas State University

Margie Mayfield
University of Victoria

Joanne R. Nurss
Georgia State University

Lloyd Ollila
University of Victoria

James Olson
Hopkins Public Schools
Hopkins, Minnesota

Edward Paradis
University of Wyoming

Kerry Quorn
Woodland Public Schools
Woodland, Washington

Kathleen Telepak
DeKalb County Schools
Decatur, Georgia

Foreword

During the past decade we have seen major changes in the purpose and content of kindergarten education, particularly the place and amount of reading instruction. During this same period the significant impact administrators have on the quality of instruction in the elementary school has received attention. This book brings both of these vital topics into focus.

The subject of reading in the kindergarten has become a debated issue for teachers, administrators, and parents. Opinions on the amount and type of reading readiness instruction and formal beginning reading instruction have ranged from a "hands-off," no instruction position to one of a highly structured, intense, beginning reading program for everyone in kindergarten. It is more and more apparent that kindergartens are being forced to make significant shifts in the content of their curriculum and the function of the teacher.

Many people feel the kindergarten child of today arrives at school much more sophisticated and better prepared to begin formal reading instruction. With the advent of smaller families, some parents often give more time and attention to the development of their children. Many of these parents are anxious for their children to have more formal reading instruction in kindergarten. Some children have had years of experience in preschools and formal nurseries. Others arrive with limited experience and little preparation for beginning reading instruction. This spread in preparation of children, coupled with the interest and concern of parents, requires that educators carefully examine the kind and amount of reading readiness instruction and formal reading instruction to be provided in the kindergarten.

Research such as that done by the Rand Corporation in Los Angeles and the Philadelphia School Systems helps us focus more clearly on the significant impact administrators, particularly principals, have on the amount of growth children make in reading. Schools which are providing quality reading instruction usually have strong educational leaders who understand the content of a comprehensive reading program. They are familiar with reading materials and how they are to be used in providing reading instruction. They motivate, coordinate, and facilitate the implementation of all phases of a broad reading program.

Principals who are well prepared provide many services to classroom teachers, ranging from consulting to assisting with instruction. They are constantly aware of and sensitive to the staff development needs of their teachers. Essentially they do everything for their teachers that they expect the teachers to do for their students.

This book, prepared for IRA's Early Childhood and Reading Development Committee, offers meaningful insight and practical suggestions on the place of reading in kindergarten and the ways administrators can assist and coordinate kindergarten reading programs. It contains scholarly reviews of the status of reading in the kindergarten and what we know about the readiness of children. Chapters are devoted to the content and organization of a kindergarten reading program and the roles administrators and teachers play in implementing that program. The book should be useful to teachers, administrators, and parents, as well as to professors and students of kindergarten education courses.

Floyd Sucher
Brigham Young University

IRA PUBLICATIONS COMMITTEE 1982-1983   Joan Nelson-Herber, State University of New York at Binghamton, *Chairing* • Phylliss J. Adams, University of Denver • Roach Van Allen, University of Arizona • Janet R. Binkley, IRA • Faye R. Branca, IRA • Martha Collins Cheek, Louisiana State University • Susan Mandel Glazer, Rider College • MaryAnne Hall, Georgia State University • Dale D. Johnson, University of Wisconsin • Martha L. King, Ohio State University • Lloyd W. Kline, IRA • Elaine P. LeBlanc, Georgia Department of Education, Atlanta • Irving P. McPhail, University of Maryland • Nancy Naumann, North Haven, Connecticut, Board of Education • Caroline Neal, West Virginia College of Graduate Studies • P. David Pearson, University of Illinois • María Elena Rodríquez, Asociacion Internacional de Lectura, Buenos Aires • Betty Roe, Tennessee Technological University • S. Jay Samuels, University of Minnesota • Ralph C. Staiger, IRA • John C. Stansell, Texas A & M University • Rosemary Winkeljohann, St. Ursula Villa Elementary School, Cincinnati.

Introduction

This book is designed to assist those who administer kindergarten reading programs. Although its primary focus is upon the principal, the handbook also contains helpful ideas for kindergarten teachers. The increasing demand for an inclusion of reading activities in the kindergarten curriculum makes it imperative that those in charge understand *how* reading can best be introduced, as well as *when* reading should be introduced.

The first chapter provides background information about the place of reading in the kindergarten program and offers some insights into various effective reading programs. Chapter Two examines typical characteristics and diversities of the five year old child. Chapter Three focuses specifically on the administrator's role in developing a kindergarten reading program and suggests ways of working with teachers and parents. Chapter Four provides guidelines for implementing a program involving reading at the kindergarten level. Chapter Five describes different patterns for organizing the reading program, and Chapter Six presents a plan for continuous diagnosis and assessment.

Kindergartens play vital roles in getting students started toward their education. The handbook for administrators and teachers is dedicated to making the kindergarten experience a good beginning in reading as well as in other areas of the curriculum.

The editor would like to acknowledge the contributions of Kathy Ollila and the Early Childhood and Reading Development Committee of the International Reading Association for their helpful suggestions and comments in developing this handbook.

LLO

Foundations:
What Have We Learned about
Kindergarten Reading Programs?

1   **Lloyd O. Ollila**

Why does an administrator need to know so much about beginning reading? Isn't teaching reading the first grade teacher's responsibility? The administrator has other duties: budgets to meet, supplies to order, parents to placate, and staffing problems to solve. All of these capacities are essential, of course, but there are very good reasons why administrators should acquire in addition a functional knowledge of beginning reading.

From 1967 to 1970 the International Reading Association's Committee on Administration and Reading conducted a program of regional and national seminars, dialogues, workshops, and institutes involving teachers, reading consultants, curriculum personnel, and school administrators. The Committee reports the following:

> Most teachers feel insecure to a substantial degree about the teaching of reading. They want guidance, encouragement, inservice training, time for planning, and relief from some of the obstacles which inhibit effective reading instruction. They feel that their principal or their superintendent has the power to help them with the reading program, and that their administrators have an obligation to exercise their power to perform the following functions: 1) To try to improve the quality of reading instruction in the classroom. 2) To establish an attitude and an atmosphere which enhances the reading program. 3) To provide optimum conditions to assist each child to learn to read. 4) To budget sufficient funds to implement an effective reading program (4:11).

Obviously, to perform all these functions effectively, administrators should be well informed about the teaching of reading.

Administrators hold key positions in coordinating beginning reading programs and they can bring primary grade teachers together to discuss and develop a free flowing program through the grades. Administrators' knowledge of beginning reading can help their school or district to avoid the pitfalls of a disjointed program. Too often teachers close their doors and tend to the business of teaching reading in their classrooms, isolated from the rest of the school's reading program. The administrator can help the teacher perceive the total picture of reading instruction as it develops throughout the school.

One common problem today, requiring a leadership thrust by administrators, has resulted from the new demands created for grade one teachers because of the introduction of reading instruction in kindergarten. Beginning reading programs frequently must be altered because of the child's previous learning, especially in schools that individualize the kindergarten program so that some children may start reading activities while other children do not. Durkin (19:60) flatly states, "Earlier starts in reading are meaningless if schools are unwilling to alter what is taught in the years that follow kindergarten." The administrator knowledgeable about beginning reading can oversee and coordinate the program so that early starts by children and past efforts of teachers are not ignored and wasted.

Unfortunately, many administrators are not knowledgeable about beginning reading. Most have never taught primary grades; many have never taught a child to read. Often, in fact, administrators have picked up whatever information on beginning reading they have from watching primary teachers in the classroom and discussing what was happening with the teacher. This approach to learning about beginning reading may have the merit of being based on classroom observations, but it is a fragmented type of observation with no grand overview of how reading skills develop. Furthermore, surveys reveal that there is often a conspicuous discrepancy between what reading experts are saying and what is actually happening in the classroom. Administrators need to venture further than their own district classrooms to understand and appreciate what goes into beginning reading.

It is not easy to become knowledgeable and aware of current happenings in beginning reading. For one thing, there is so very much happening. Reading is professed to be the most widely researched field in education. The sheer quantity of reading publications is overwhelming. Aukerman (3) reports that there are more than a hundred beginning reading approaches available to teachers. The publication of reading textbooks, workbooks, games, and hardware is a fiercely competitive multimillion dollar industry turning out hundreds of new items every year. Since the early sixties, materials for reading readiness and beginning reading have comprised a large part of this production. An educator first delving into the field can easily be overwhelmed by the numerous research studies, technical developments, innovative trends, and quantity of materials available. It is a real problem for school administrators and teachers to sift through and find programs, materials, and techniques that will work best for their particular pupils. This problem is compounded by inflation and tighter budgets which command school personnel to make wise and careful selections of reading materials because they likely will have to be used for a long time.

This booklet is designed to help busy administrators to become acquainted with current research and the changes, thoughts, and happenings in beginning reading. Although in this book much of the knowledge about beginning reading is summarized for the sake of brevity, the authors include further reading references so that the reader may pursue topics of particular interest. This booklet also discusses the administrator's role in developing a sound beginning reading program—a program in which children not only learn to read but learn to enjoy reading.

Definition of Reading

Reading is a specialized, complex, and personal task. Since authorities define reading in a variety of ways, confusion and controversy often result. Some reading textbook authors have avoided the problem altogether. yet it is important for the administrator to develop his own conception of reading. Without it, formulating the objectives of a reading program is hazardous. How can an administrator help reading teachers to evaluate their students' reading skills, diagnose their reading strengths and weaknesses, and select strategies for remediation in reading with no clear concept of *reading*?

Because reading authorities have defined reading in differing ways, the educator must make some choices in deciding what his own definition should be. Broadly speaking, reading definitions fall into "code emphasis" and "meaning emphasis" conceptions (10). Bloomfield and Barnhart (6) provide an example of code emphasis: "Reading involves nothing more than the correlation of a sound image with its corresponding visual image." This view stresses reading as an act of decoding printed words into spoken words and would suggest that a child should begin to read by sounding words by phonic units and then blending the sounds together, such as in the Lippincott and Distar programs. In contrast, meaning emphasis definitions minimize this aspect and stress comprehension as the major component of reading. For example, Artley (2) defines reading as "the art of reconstructing from the printed page the writer's ideas, feelings, moods, and sensory impressions." Following this definition, a child would begin to read with materials designed to help children think about what they read. Decoding word skills would be initiated later after children had memorized a number of sight words. Heavy emphasis would be put on the child's understanding and ability to interpret what he reads. Many standard basal reading series, such as those by Ginn, Houghton Mifflin, and Macmillan, would be considered as meaning emphasis programs.

Meaning and decoding are both basic components of reading. But are they the only ones? There are additional ways of viewing reading. Other writers incorporate both these components and expand the reading definition still further. For instance, Clymer (*13:28*) cites four major outcomes of the reading program: "a) decoding, which corresponds to . . . 'word perception'; b) grasping the author's meaning . . . 'literal interpretation'; c) testing and recombining the author's message with the understanding and background of the reader; d) application of ideas and values to decisions and actions and extensions of author ideas to new settings."

Spache and Spache (*39*) expand the list to seven components to describe reading. They explore and detail reading as skill development, a visual act, a perceptual act, a reflection of cultural background, a thinking process, information processing, and associational learning. Administrators should contemplate these and other definitions—perhaps, find one that corresponds with or fulfills their views of what reading is. Then again, administrators may wish to formulate or revise their own definitions. Following this, they should put their definitions in writing to help focus their search for knowledge about reading.

Definition of Reading Readiness

Children learn skills, such as how to bat balls, ride bikes, and swim, when they are ready to undertake these learning tasks—just as they do with other kinds of skill development, including reading. *Reading readiness* refers to that time when children are ready to being reading print. As Downing and Thackray (*16:9*) expand the definition, it is a time "when the child can learn easily and without emotional strain, and secondly, when the child can learn profitably because efforts at teaching give gratifying results." Readiness is not something that suddenly appears like a first tooth. Preparation for reading grows slowly as children, from ages one to four years, begin to use language, develop coordination, acquire visual and auditory skills, and expand their backgrounds of experience. All these abilities help children to get ready to read. On coming to school, a few children are ready to read but most others will need further preparation.

Not too many years ago teachers and reading experts felt that children would be ready to read if they were simply given time to mature. However, numerous studies show that teachers can teach skills that help to develop readiness to read. Today, reading authorities regard reading readiness as a match between children and the reading programs into which they are initiated. Durkin states this well in *Teaching Them to Read* (*21:162*):

> The question of a child's readiness for reading has a twofold focus: a) his capacity (a product of an interplay among genetic endowment,

maturation, experiences, and learnings) in relation to b) particular instruction that will be available.

Following this view, children could be ready to read in one school's reading program but might not be ready for another more difficult school program. Teachers can do much to accelerate children's readiness to read by modifying and adapting reading programs to fit their skills and/or by teaching the children those prerequisite skills necessary to begin the reading program. Teachers match the programs to the children and the children to the programs.

Reading readiness is also used to refer to activities and materials for helping to prepare children for reading. For instance, matching letters and finding objects that start with the same beginning sounds are generally considered part of readiness skill instruction.

In perspective, reading readiness should be viewed as part of a continuum in reading: "Readiness skills are reading, only in a very gross manner, and with continued and refined practice, reading skills will gradually become more highly complex, varied, and meaningful" (31). Although early reading skills are usually divided between readiness and reading activities, the division is arbitrary. It is helpful to some but confusing to others. For instance, what some teachers may consider to be reading readiness activities may be regarded as reading activities to others. Nonetheless, readiness remains a valuable concept because it reminds teachers that there is often a gap between what the teacher wants to teach and the child's ability to understand. Teachers can bridge the gap by simplifying the instruction and helping improve the child's understanding through the use of intermediate steps.

Modern Changes in the Kindergarten

Until the early sixties, most schools in North America neatly placed reading as a subject to begin in first grade. Grade one teachers spent the first three months helping children get ready to read and then introduced formal reading instruction. Reading instruction did not begin in kindergarten. The kindergarten teacher did some indirect preparation for reading in the form of guiding language, social and emotional development, and helping to expand the children's experiences. However, there was no deliberate, systematic, sequential program for developing prereading skills. Usually, no help was given even if some children could read prior to kindergarten or showed high aptitudes and interests in reading. Teaching initial reading was the exclusive job of the grade one teacher.

Today, teaching readiness and reading skills in kindergarten is no longer taboo. The pressure for this change came from many sources during the past decade. The jolt to the educational system began when Russia launched Sputnik and continued with the writing of Bruner (8) and Hunt (25). Further impetus was provided when O.K. Moore (29) experimented with teaching three year olds to read and Brzeninski (9) reported the Denver study of mass prereading instruction to kindergartners. Durkin's study (18) of preschool readers, plus the popularization of books like *Teach Your Baby to Read* (15), contributed to the demand that more could be taught earlier in the schools. Administrators and kindergarten teachers reacted to the pressures, and parental demand began to include reading readiness programs and, in some cases, formal reading instruction in kindergarten.

During this time, also, there were some changes in the early childhood experiences of kindergarten beginners. For many children today, kindergarten is not their first experience with school. Some children have gone to nursery school; some have attended Head Start; others have gone to day care centers where they have stayed all day while both parents worked. These children have learned to manage by themselves away from home and, to a certain extent, have adapted to socializing with others of the same age. Many of the experiences kindergartners of yesterday first tasted on coming to school are "old stuff" to their more experienced, sophisticated counterparts of today. Furthermore, the background of experiences and vocabulary of today's children is greater, thanks to television and society's mobility. From a review of the research on children's language, Hillerich (24:21) suggests "Children today are ready [for reading] about a year sooner if vocabulary development is the criterion for instruction."

Many children today have had a greater variety of experiences and opportunities open to them. On the other hand, there are some children who have not taken advantage of these opportunities, either from choice or from inability to do so. Some have never been in Head Start, watched "Sesame Street," or been read to and talked to frequently by adults. These children come to kindergarten, too. Thus, in today's kindergarten classroom, teachers face a much broader range of abilities, backgrounds of experience, and interests than was the case before the 1960s.

The Current Scene in Kindergarten

How has the kindergarten reacted to this modern child and the demand that a systematic reading readiness and/or reading program be added to the curriculum? Current surveys (11, 28) show that most kindergarten teachers today provide instruction in reading readiness. Some of these go beyond readiness and begin formal reading programs. Ching (11) reports that 25 percent of the teachers who gave instruction in readiness skills also taught reading to kindergarten children. Although most kindergarten teachers agree that those children who are ready to read or can already read should be taught, there are others who still do not provide for it. One teacher comments:

"Yes, I realize that some children are ready to read in kindergarten, but these children are definitely in the minority. My job, as I see it, is to teach to the majority of the children; and the majority in my opinion are not ready to read" (28:382).

Reading readiness and reading programs are diverse—varying greatly in organization, content, method, and materials. LaConte (28) reports that in one in three kindergarten classrooms the teacher uses experience charts, classroom libraries, stencils for development of visual perception, a reading readiness text and workbook, and an alphabet chart. She points out that the use of basal readers is rare at this level, but basal series readiness materials are commonly used. Although many kindergarten teachers do give some individualized or small group instruction, there is a greater tendency to teach readiness skills by whole class instruction.

Greater Involvement of Kindergarten Parents in the Reading Program

In many kindergarten prereading and reading programs, parents are asked to take an active part. Teachers reason that parents can support school learning and help prepare their children for reading. Schools have involved parents in a variety of educational, observational, and participation programs. Some schools send out newsletters with explanations of their kindergarten reading programs, or they hold open houses to explain their programs. Sometimes teachers advise parents that certain prereading skills will be taught and then give parents suggestions for support and follow-up activities at home (32). Some commercial prereading programs such as Macmillan's include a set of letters to parents which teachers can mimeograph and send to parents. Besides newsletters, many teachers try to get together with large and small groups of parents to discuss and demonstrate what is being done in school. For instance, a teacher might show the parents how to read a story aloud by reading and discussing the story with several of the children from the class. Breiling (7:187) reported in "Using Parents as Teaching Partners" that parents were enthusiastic and most believed that their children became more interested in reading. Details of these meetings are indicated through comments such as: "It has helped me to work better with my child. It has stimulated my interest as well as hers. I wish something of this type had been available years ago for my older children who lost interest in school by junior high."

Other Current Practices in the Kindergarten

In many kindergartens today, a battery of reading correlated tests is given to each child in an attempt to get an early identification of those who might experience difficulty learning to read. This battery should include both standardized and informal teacher-developed tests. It is hoped that the teacher, knowing such potential problem children, will be able to develop and implement a program to correct those learning deficits disclosed and give the child a better chance of success in learning to read. These tests help the teacher diagnose each child's strengths and weaknesses and individualize the readiness/reading program. Such tests are a major part of early identification programs. Although they can, to some extent, predict reading success or failure, this information should be used to improve the child's chances for success rather than to label the child. More information about these tests appears in Chapter Six.

Another common practice in kindergartens today is the use of transition rooms. Transition rooms combine some activities from kindergarten with some activities from grade one. They provide an intermediate step for those children who complete kindergarten but are not yet ready for a more formally structured academic grade one program. Some children need more language development and preparation for reading, more liberal play time, and more time to "grow up" than can be given in grade one. These children are not necessarily mentally slow; they may just need more time to adjust to the work requirements of school. For these children the transition room with its smaller classes and slower pacing of instruction is ideal.

Many kindergartens employ teacher aides or get parents or other volunteers to help the teacher with the program. Typically, aides take on the noninstructional classroom jobs—such as preparing bulletin boards, supervising art projects, and generally helping the children— while the teacher is giving small group or individual instruction. Aides are well liked by the teachers since they conserve the teacher's professional time so that it can be devoted to educational concerns, such as individualizing instruction, instead of being wasted on nonteaching tasks.

What Does Research Say about Teaching Reading in the Kindergarten?

Current surveys and observations reveal that a sizable group of teachers is beginning reading in the form of instruction in printing and naming letters, discriminating between letter sounds, completing exercises in readiness workbooks, and developing a key sight vocabulary. Research studies such as those of Clark (*12*), Durkin (*19*), and Plessas and Oakes (*34*) have found that a small proportion of children has learned to read before kindergarten. Teachers should help these children to increase their reading abilities, but the majority of children who come to kindergarten are unable to read and require different programs. Effective readiness or reading activities must be provided based on each child's capabilities. In ensuing paragraphs, four main conclusions are summarized from research on this skill training.

1. *Children can be taught readiness skills.* Many studies conclude that planned readiness training is possible and profitable for kindergartners. For instance, this writer (*30*) reviewed seventeen original research studies on visual discrimination training alone, finding that, to a certain extent, skill in visual discrimination can be improved by direct training at the kindergarten level. Hillerich (*23*) conducted a study to determine, among other things, whether kindergartners could master prereading skills involving the use of oral context and consonant-letter sound association to read printed words. From data on 363 children, Hillerich found that 70 percent of the kindergartners could master these skills by the end of the year. At the beginning of September of their grade one year, Hillerich repeated the same test to see how many of the skills would still be retained and found that most of the children remembered what they had learned the previous year. On the average, there was a small loss of only 2.6 points on the fifty-eight item test.

2. *For many kindergarten children, readiness training improves their readiness for reading and, therefore, their chances for later success in beginning reading programs.* Research demonstrates that this conclusion is particularly true for kindergarten children with language differences resulting from lower socioeconomic environments or culturally disadvantaged backgrounds. Stanchfield (*40*) developed an intensive readiness program for teaching skills including training in 1) listening for comprehension of content, 2) listening for auditory discrimination, 3) visual discrimination skills, 4) oral language skills, 5) motor-perceptual skills, and 6) sound-symbol correspondence. Black, Chicano, and white kindergarten children from seventeen American schools participated in the study. The experimental group having this training developed significantly more reading readiness skills as judged by readiness tests than the children in regular kindergarten programs. Spache (*38*) reports similar results in a study with lower socioeconomic and linguistically different black children.

Logically, readiness training seems to be beneficial to those most lacking in skills, but it has been shown to be valuable for others also. In the Denver study reported by Brzeinski (*9*) a cross section of 4,000 kindergartners was given systematic instruction including learning the letters of the alphabet and the sounds represented by them and the use of context with sounds and displayed words. By the end of grade one the children given such instruction in kindergarten were better readers than those in the control group who did not receive that instruction. Hillerich (*23*) directed a similar study, teaching many of the same skills to 363 children. Again the children with prior, systematic readiness training in kindergarten were reading significantly better than the control group by the end of grade one (even though the control group, with a regular kindergarten program was of slightly higher academic ability). Other studies (5, 35) also conclude that readiness training enhances success in beginning reading.

3. *What skills should be included in readiness training programs?* A number of factors (including general health and maturity, sex, mental age and intelligence, neurological conditions, vision, speech, hearing, cultural and socioeconomic backgrounds, emotional and personality factors, motivation, perceptual abilities affecting visual and auditory discrimination, conceptual development, perceptual motor skills, and language facility) have been correlated with success in beginning reading. Although reading experts have found these factors to be related to reading, this fact does not mean that one guarantees the other or that without facility in any single factor a child will not be able to read. The teacher has little or no control over some of these factors. Other factors can be improved through training and are commonly included in readiness programs.

The skills to be included in a readiness program are dependent on both the children and the reading programs used. No reading authority can prescribe a program that will be necessary for all children to follow. In spite of this, numerous publishers have brought out readiness workbooks designed to teach skills necessary to begin reading. Allen (1) analyzed a number of readiness workbooks and listed their activities in order of frequency: 1) language development using sequential pictures; 2) visual discrimination using the matching of common pictures, objects, geometric forms, letters, and words; 3) motor training by tracing, copying, and drawing dot pictures and mazes; 4) auditory training with common sounds, rhyming, and initial consonants; and 5) discrimination of outlines of shapes or words. Children weak in any of these skills may profit from parts of these workbooks; however, the workbooks must be used in perspective as an optional part instead of as the whole readiness program.

Other skills can be taught and should not be overlooked just because they are not commonly included in readiness workbooks. For instance, children need to learn to pay attention during group instruction, a skill basic not only to reading but to all school progress.

4. *Some kinds of skill training are more valuable than others.* Several researchers have questioned the validity of training kindergarten children in certain readiness skills. Klesius (27) reports the results of eleven studies investigating the influence of perceptual motor development programs upon reading. He found the results of these studies contradictory. Whether children's readiness to read will be furthered by training programs as suggested by Delacato (36) and Frostig (23) is questionable; and Klesius suggests that if perceptual

motor training programs are used, they should be used in a supplementary capacity.

There are several commercial programs devoted to developing visual perception. Paradis (33) concludes that the value of using these whole programs in readiness training is questionable. Ollila (30) compared three commercial readiness programs in his study with kindergartners and found that no one training program was more effective than the other programs in teaching the skills of auditory and visual discrimination. This finding was of special interest considering that one of the programs was designed specifically to develop visual perception and did not include any exercises for the development of auditory discrimination skills. Findings such as these should warn teachers and administrators to be careful in selecting readiness training programs. Is the training making children more ready for reading? Could parts of the training be dropped or supplemented by other more effective training? Teaching time is too precious to waste on activities that have little or no value.

Studies of Formal Reading in Kindergarten

1. *Can formal reading be taught in kindergarten, and does this earlier introduction serve a worthwhile purpose?* There are a number of studies and experiments in which four year olds and kindergartners were given systematic instruction that went beyond prereading skills. These studies show that young children can be taught to read. For example, Sutton (42) taught a selected group of children to read in kindergarten. Then she followed their reading achievement through grade three. She found that at the end of grade three the early readers maintained consistently higher scores than others not involved in the program. Other studies [done by Kelley (26) and cited by Downing and Thackray (16)], in which reading was taught in kindergarten, have proved to be more interesting in that Kelley's pilot and subsequent study used different methods and produced some interesting and provocative results. In her pilot program Kelley included only those children who wished to read; children who expressed no interest or did not want to read were excluded. By second grade, the earlier readers were better readers with better attitudes toward reading than their later starting counterparts. In a later experiment, Kelley divided two comparable sets of kindergartners into control and experimental groups and reported that the experiment "...frustrated some bright children in the control group who wished to read and some others in the experimental group who did not want to read. While it was nearly possible to keep the lid on the control group, it was virtually impossible to teach some children in the experimental group to read" (p. 69). Teaching formal reading skills to a selected group of interested

kindergartners is one thing, but trying to teach children who do not wish to learn and who haven't developed basic prereading skills could result in wasted effort.

2. *Although formal reading can be taught to some children, the question remains of whether the earlier start will result in just temporary gains or long term greater achievement in school work.* Durkin (*19*) conducted a six year study of children who learned to read in school at the age of four. She first devised a two-year pre-first grade language arts program (described later in this chapter) using many of the findings from her earlier studies of preschool home readers. Thirty-seven four year old volunteers were taught via this program, and their subsequent reading achievements during grades one to four were compared with the reading attainments of a control group of classmates. This control group had not been part of the experimental program but had attended kindergarten where some readiness instruction (numeral and letter naming, development of a small reading vocabulary) was given. Durkin reasoned that the earlier start of the experimental group should make these children better readers. This assumption seemed to hold true, as throughout grades one to four the early readers' reading achievements exceeded that of the control group (although in grades three and four the differences were not statistically significant). During the grade one to four years of the experiment, Durkin's great expectations for the early reader's progress were diminished by her observations of classroom practice. In one visit, a second grade teacher spent sixty minutes teaching reading—ten minutes with the higher achievers and fifty minutes with five children reading below grade level. In other visits, she noted teachers strictly following the basals, disregarding other reading methods, always religiously beginning the year with the first level basal of that year, regardless of the reading levels of the children. From these and other questionable practices, Durkin concluded that early reading should be started only in schools "in which all faculty members and the administration are committed to a reading program in which instruction is matched to children's current achievements, not to a designated basal reader or to a grade level sign on a classroom door" (p. 59). She believes, as stated previously, early starts are "meaningless" if administrators and teachers will not commit themselves to altering their teaching practices to fit the needs of the earlier readers.

From Durkin's experience with the longitudinal study and experimental prefirst grade language arts program comes the following guideline for teachers and administrators (*19*:60):

> Since there is no guarantee that a kindergarten start in reading will lead to greater success in future years, no school should introduce reading instruction into its kindergartens unless that instruction can be of a kind

that will add both enjoyment and greater self-esteem to the fifth year of the child's life. This recommendation stands in great contrast to some current school practices in which reading is being introduced with nothing but whole-class instruction characterized for the most part by drill and rote learning.

3. *How should beginning reading skills be taught in kindergarten?* Little help in answering this question can be drawn from the numerous studies comparing formal and informal beginning reading programs. A formal program can be characterized as a systematic, structured sequence of skillbuilding activities. The trend in many kindergartens throughout North America is to adopt some form of formal program for teaching readiness skills. Reading researchers and writers have voiced their concern over poorly conceived translations of formal programs—the no-nonsense pencil pushing, the workbook-oriented mass instruction approach, and the watered-down grade one impression. Despite the many pitfalls to formal programs, there are far more research studies showing the effectiveness of the early formal skill training than those discounting it. Studies by Brzeinski (9), Hillerich (23), and Stanchfield (40) find structured programs more effective. An informal program, while teaching the same skills as a formal program, is relatively unstructured with teacher-designed activity or experience units. Studies, such as that by Blakely and Shadle (5), favor informal programs at a kindergarten level. A third group of studies comparing informal and formal programs (35, 14, 37) finds no significant differences between formal and informal readiness programs.

Moving on from the contradictory evidence comparing formal and informal programs, other researchers have looked at characteristics of early readers who learned to read prior to school entrance. The researchers studied how these children learned to read and looked for common patterns that could provide ideas for helping beginning readers. Plessas and Oakes (34) studied forty children who were able to read at primer level or above upon entering grade one. The children showed an early personal interest in print and in wanting to read signs, and they had many questions about words and letters. They were living in homes which encouraged many activities related to reading. Their parents or siblings were willing to help with reading problems and questions.

Durkin (18) carried on a longitudinal study with forty-nine children who learned to read between the ages of three and five. These children, too, had willing adults and/or brothers and sisters available to answer their questions about reading. Parents provided books, chalk boards, paper, and pencils as requested. Many children showed their first interest in reading through writing. The children showed an early interest in written language—some wanting to print, others wanting to know what signs and magazines said. Parents of these children like to read themselves and often read to their children. Durkin points out that most parents do not deliberately attempt to teach their children to read. Instead, parents seem to follow the interests of the child and respond to them. Durkin feels the schools can learn much from how these early readers learned to read. She characterizes this method as a "language arts approach." She would have the kindergarten include in its curriculum many of the characteristics of the language arts approach as described in *The Kindergarten Child and Reading* (20:3): "Stimulating growth in both oral and written language abilities were various combinations of 1) interesting experiences; 2) opportunities to discuss and ask questions; 3) availability of one or more persons to respond to questions and requests related to reading, writing, and spelling; 4) availability of materials for writing; 5) positive contacts with books and reading; 6) displays of written words and numbers that related to the children's interests (birthdays, television, programs, games)."

In 1977 a number of educators representing various professional organizations* concerned with early childhood education wrote a joint statement of concerns about present practices and recommendations for improvement in pre-first grade reading instruction (*41*). This statement in its entirety follows.

A PERSPECTIVE ON PRE-FIRST GRADERS AND THE TEACHING OF READING

Pre-first graders need...

opportunities to express orally, graphically, and dramatically their feelings and responses to experiences.

opportunities to interpret the language of others whether it is written, spoken, or nonverbal.

Teachers of pre-first graders need...

preparation which emphasizes developmentally appropriate language experiences for all pre-first graders, including those ready to read or already reading.

the combined efforts of professional organizations, colleges, and universities to help them successfully meet the concerns outlined in this document.

CONCERNS

1. A growing number of children are enrolled in pre-kindergarten and kindergarten classes in which highly structured prereading and reading programs are being used.

---

*Dorothy Strickland, Dolores Durkin, Joanne Nurss, Lloyd Ollila (IRA); Jessie Roderick (NCTE); Jeanne Corbin, Virginia Plunkett (AAE/K/NE); Dell Kjer, Alberta Meyer, (ACEI); Barbara Day (ASCD); William Pharis (NAESP); Georgianna Engstrom, Marilyn Smith (YAEYC).

2. Decisions related to schooling, including the teaching of reading, are increasingly being made on economic and political bases instead of on our knowledge of young children and of how they best learn.

3. In a time of diminishing financial resources, schools often try to make "a good showing" on measures of achievement that may or may not be appropriate for the children involved. Such measures all too often dictate the content and goals of the programs.

4. In attempting to respond to pressures for high scores on widely-used measures of achievement, teachers of young children sometimes feel compelled to use materials, methods, and activities designed for older children. In so doing, they may impede the development of intellectual functions such as curiosity, critical thinking, and creative expression, and, at the same time, promote negative attitudes toward reading.

5. A need exists to provide alternative ways to teach and evaluate progress in prereading and reading skills.

6. Teachers of pre-first graders who are carrying out highly individualized programs without depending upon commercial readers and workbooks need help in articulating for themselves and the public *what* they are doing and *why*.

RECOMMENDATIONS

1. Provide reading experiences as an integrated part of the broader communication process that includes listening, speaking, and writing. A language experience approach is an example of such integration.

2. Provide for a broad range of activities both in scope and in content. Include direct experiences that offer opportunities to communicate in different settings with different persons.

3. Foster children's affective and cognitive development by providing materials, experiences, and opportunities to communicate what they know and how they feel.

4. Continually appraise how various aspects of each child's total development affects his/her reading development.

5. Use evaluative procedures that are developmentally appropriate for the children being assessed and that reflect the goals and objectives of the instructional program.

6. Insure feelings of success for all children in order to help them see themselves as persons who can enjoy exploring language and learning to read.

7. Plan flexibly in order to accommodate a variety of learning styles and ways of thinking.

8. Respect the language the child brings to school, and use it as a base for language activities.

9. Plan activities that will cause children to become active participants in the learning process rather than passive recipients of knowledge.

10. Provide opportunities for children to experiment with language and simply to have fun with it.

11. Require that preservice and inservice teachers of young children be prepared in the teaching of reading in a way that emphasizes reading as an integral part of the language arts as well as the total curriculum.

12. Encourage developmentally appropriate language learning opportunities in the home.

Conclusion

Administrators should ensure that the kindergarten program is related to the total school program. They should see that the teacher provides a proper balance of reading for those who are able and additional preparation for those who require it. A transition room should be established if numbers warrant it. The administrator must be careful to hire and/or encourage kindergarten teachers who have a basic foundation in reading and language development. If tenured teachers have little or no such background, they should be encouraged to upgrade themselves by taking necessary course work and attending inservice courses that will improve their skills.

References

1. Allen, R.J., et al. "The Relationship of Readiness Factors to January First Grade Reading Achievement," master's thesis, Boston University, 1959.
2. Artley, A.S. *What is Reading?* Chicago: Scott, Foresman, 1961.
3. Aukerman, R. *Approaches to Beginning Reading.* New York: John Wiley and Sons, 1971.
4. Avery, P.J. "The Obligations of School Administrators to the Reading Program," in T. R. Carlson (Ed.), *Administrators and Reading.* New York: Harcourt Brace Jovanovich, 1972.
5. Blakely, W.P., and E.M. Shadle. "A Study of Two Readiness-for-Reading Programs in Kindergarten," *Elementary English,* 38 (1961), 502-505.
6. Bloomfield, L., and C.L. Barnhart. *Let's Read: A Linguistic Approach.* Detroit: Wayne State University Press, 1961.
7. Breiling, A. "Using Parents as Teaching Partners," *Reading Teacher,* 30 (November 1976), 187.
8. Bruner, J.S. *The Process of Education.* Cambridge, Massachusetts: Harvard University Press, 1960.
9. Brzeinski, J.B. *Summary Report of the Effectiveness of Teaching Reading in the Denver Public Schools,* Cooperative Project No. 5-0371. Denver.
10. Chall, J. *Learning to Read: The Great Debate.* New York: McGraw-Hill, 1967.
11. Ching, D. "The Teaching of Reading in Kindergarten," paper presented at the International Reading Association Convention, Anaheim, California, 1970.
12. Clark, M. *Young Fluent Readers.* London: Heinemann Educational Books, 1976.
13. Clymer, T. "What is Reading? Some Current Concepts," *Innovation and Change in Reading Instruction,* 67th Yearbook of the National Society for the Study of Education, Part II. Chicago: University of Chicago Press, 1968.
14. Collins, M.E. "Determining the Relative Efficiency of a Particular Reading Readiness Workbook: A Teacher Developed Program in Promoting Reading Readiness," unpublished master's thesis, DePauw University, 1960.
15. Doman, G. *How to Teach Your Baby to Read.* New York: Random House, 1964.
16. Downing, J., and D. Thackray. *Reading Readiness,* Second Edition, a UKRA Teaching of Reading Monograph. London: Hodder and Stoughton, 1975.
17. Durkin, D. "A Study of Children Who Learned to Read Prior to First Grade," *California Journal of Educational Research,* 10 (1959), 109-113.
18. Durkin, D. *Children Who Read Early.* New York: Teachers College Press, Columbia University, 1966.
19. Durkin, D. "A Six Year Study of Children Who Learned to Read in School at the Age of Four," *Reading Research Quarterly,* 10 (1974-1975).

20. Durkin, D. "Facts about Prefirst Grade Reading," in L. Ollila (Ed.), *The Kindergarten Child and Reading*. Newark, Delaware: International Reading Association, 1977, 1-12.
21. Durkin, D. *Teaching Them to Read*, Third Edition. Boston: Allyn and Bacon, 1978.
22. Frostig, M., and D. Home. *The Frostig Program for the Development of Visual Perception*. Chicago: Follett, 1964.
23. Hillerich, R.L. "Prereading Skills in Kindergarten: A Second Report," *Elementary School Journal*, 65 (1965), 312-317.
24. Hillerich, R.L. *Reading Fundamentals for Preschool and Primary Children*. Columbus, Ohio: Charles E. Merrill, 1977.
25. Hunt, J. *Intelligence and Experience*. New York: Ronald Press, 1961.
26. Kelley, M.L. "Reading in the Kindergarten," in J.A. Figurel (Ed.), *Reading and Inquiry*. Newark, Delaware: International Reading Association, 1965.
27. Klesius, S.E. "Perceptual Motor Development and Reading: A Closer Look," in R.C. Aukerman (Ed.), *Some Persistent Questions on Beginning Reading*. Newark, Delaware: International Reading Association, 1972.
28. LaConte, C. "Reading in the Kindergarten: Fact or Fantasy?" *Elementary English*, 47 (1970), 382-387.
29. Moore, O.K. "O.K.'s Children," *Time*, 76 (November 7, 1960), 103.
30. Ollila, L. "The Effects of Three Contrasting Readiness Programs on the Readiness Skill of Kindergarten Boys and Girls," unpublished doctoral dissertation, 1970.
31. Ollila, L., J. Dey, and K. Ollila. "What is the Function of Kindergarten Reading Materials?" in L. Ollila (Ed.), *The Kindergarten Child and Reading*. Newark, Delaware: International Reading Association, 1977.
32. Ollila, K., and L. Ollila. "Training Parents to Help Their Children at Home," *Prime Areas*, Journal of the B.C. Primary Association, 21 (1979).
33. Paradis, E.E. "The Appropriateness of Visual Discrimination Exercises in Reading Readiness Materials," *Journal of Educational Research*, 67 (1974).
34. Plessas, G.P., and C.R. Oakes. "Prereading Experiences of Selected Early Readers," *Reading Teacher*, 17 (1964), 241-245.
35. Ploghoft, M.H. "Do Reading Readiness Workbooks Promote Readiness?" *Elementary English*, 36 (1959), 424-426.
36. Robbins, M. "Delacato Interpretation of Neurological Organization," *Reading Research Quarterly*, 1 (1966), 57-78.
37. Silberberg, M.C. "The Effect of Formal Reading Readiness Training in Kindergarten on Development of Readiness Skills and Growth in Reading," unpublished doctoral dissertation, University of Minnesota, 1966.
38. Spache, G.D., et al. *A Longitudinal First Grade Reading Readiness Program*. Cooperative Research Project No. 2742. Tallahassee, Florida: State Department of Education, 1965.
39. Spache, G.D., and E.B. Spache. *Reading in the Elementary School*, Fourth Edition. Boston: Allyn and Bacon, 1977.
40. Stanchfield, J.M. "The Development of Prereading Skills in an Experimental Kindergarten Program," *Elementary School Journal*, 8 (1971), 438-447.
41. Strickland, D., et al. "Reading and Prefirst Grade," *Reading Teacher*, 30 (1977), 780-781.
42. Sutton, M.H. "Children Who Learned to Read in Kindergarten: A Longitudinal Study," *Reading Teacher*, 22 (1969), 595-602.

Understanding New Perspectives of Early Childhood:
What Does Research Tell Us about Children?

2

John Downing
Sara Lundsteen

This chapter provides administrators with an up-to-the-minute picture of where basic research in psychology and linguistics has arrived on questions of reading readiness. Many of the studies cited here, therefore, are quite recent and as yet not universally known. However, older studies also are reviewed if their findings still remain the last word on a particular problem. Considered first are the following psychological aspects of early childhood development as they influence readiness for learning to read: the physiology of eyes and ears and the relationship with visual and auditory perception, conceptual learning and reasoning processes, and a number of other influences on child development of knowledge about the reading process. A description follows on how children's oral language develops in relation to beginning reading.

Physiological and Perceptual Factors

Common sense indicates that eyes and ears in normal children are essential for learning to read. One needs vision to see print and one needs hearing to hear the sounds of language that are related to the printed symbols. The relationship between children's visual and auditory abilities and the process of learning to read, however, is much more complex than it may seem.

First of all, one must distinguish between the sensory mechanisms of the eye and the ear and the perceptual processes in which the sensations from eyes and ears are interpreted by the brain.

The Eyes and Visual Perception

Downing and Thackray (26) reviewed the older research on the relationship between visual defects and failure in reading and found that there was little agreement among different investigators as to any causal connection between poor sight and poor reading. Nevertheless, "All investigators feel that it is important to make an early check on children's vision and to keep close watch on their progress in the early stages of reading" (p. 31). This precaution seems even more justified in the light of more recent research by Bedwell (3). His studies using the more sophisticated technology of modern ocular measuring equipment indicate that, in many cases, there is a connection between reading disability and visual defects. Moreover, his reports show how teachers can detect visual problems that can be treated by qualified specialists. For example, Bedwell states: "If children are observed when reading or working at their desks, signs of ocular stress can sometimes be noticed. Common instances are general appearance of tension, including frowning, screwing up the eyes, and excessive blinking" (p. 80). Posture may also indicate a vision problem. Bedwell notes that, "In any class, children will have very many different attitudes of posture. Sometimes a fixed trend will be evident, in another case the child may appear almost to be searching for a suitable position, for example, a child may have his head on one side, or even rest the side of his head on his desk" (p. 75). Another observable symptom of eye problems is "a considerable degree of head movement while reading. If this is combined with difficulty in maintaining coordination of the eyes, movement of the head can be associated with a tendency to switch to use one eye more than the other, and possibly back again" (p. 75).

Teachers who observe such symptoms should find ways of helping the child to obtain a proper diagnosis from a competent professional eye specialist. The usual visual screening tests in school fail to detect these deficiencies. Their diagnosis and treatment require considerable experience and sophisticated equipment.

Although serious harm can be done by forcing children who are suffering from such visual anomalies to read, according to Shaw (82), the eyes of the normal child are sufficiently well developed at the age of twelve months to handle the task of reading.

Given that children's eyes are physiologically and functionally healthy, there still remains the question of visual *perception*. The question then is: Can children intelligently interpret the visual stimuli to which they are exposed? For example, can children discriminate between small differences in shapes and their orientations such as those that occur in letters of the alphabet? As Durell (28) puts it, "If the child cannot tell letters apart, it is futile for the teacher to teach him words." This conclusion seems obvious, but if children cannot tell letters apart, one must ask: Why not? Do children have some fundamental deficiency in discriminating among *all* kinds of visible shapes or do they have problems *only with letters*?

Researchers have tried to distinguish between these two types of perceptual defects. Diagnostically, the difference has potential significance for treatment. Most studies, however, have found low correlations between reading success and visual perception when the perceptual tests did not consist of printed letters or words. But, if the visual perception test has been one in which printed letters or words are used, correlations have usually been quite high (.5 to .6). Indeed, the kindergarten test that has proved to be the best single predictor of reading achievement in first grade is one in which children must indicate which letter the examiner names (40, 66, 71). To do well in this test, children must know the name of the letter as well as be able to discriminate its shape from other letters. As Piaget (76) has shown, children learn names for things *after* they have learned to discriminate them. Thus, if children can recognize a letter by name, they have reached a high level of confidence in their own abilities to perceive its shape. However, if the children have simply been taught the names of letters by rote instruction, this type of test becomes of no predictive value (80). The reason for the uselessness of teaching children the names of letters is classified later in the discussion on Cognitive Factors.

Although correlations between reading success and non-letter/non-word tests of visual discrimination have been found to be low, some authors have developed training procedures for this type of visual discrimination ability. The procedures have not been successful in regular kindergarten programs. For example, various researchers (68, 47, ·100) have found that the Frostig (36) Program for the Development of Visual Perception has little, if any, effect on early reading instruction. The review of these types of training programs by Downing and Thackray led them to conclude (26:76): "Before engaging in a programme to change the child to fit him better for the reading task, we should be sure that the change really will make him more ready for reading."

In summary, research shows that most children come to kindergarten with eyes capable of coping with the tasks of reading, but children vary considerably in their abilities to discriminate between the visible shapes of printed letters and words. Children who are poor in discriminating between letter and word shapes should be trained in discriminating between letter and word shapes—not in other shapes.

The Ears and Auditory Perception

Research tells a similar story in regard to hearing. Downing and Thackray (26) reviewed the evidence on the connection between hearing and learning to read and concluded "given a degree of hearing sufficient to enable the child to join in the activities of the ordinary classroom, then auditory acuity is not closely related to success in reading." Nevertheless, serious hearing defects do cause difficulties in learning to read, especially if the teaching method relies heavily on phonic instruction. One type of hearing deficiency known to be a particularly serious cause of problems under such conditions is high frequenty impairment, in which children are unable to distinguish sounds such as those at the beginning of words like *sin, fin, thin.* Teachers should watch for signs of hearing impairment and try to find ways for children to receive expert diagnosis and treatment.

In this connection, it should be noted that several investigations have found that certain speech defects are related to difficulties in learning to read (39). If children are unable to articulate particular speech sounds, they may find it difficult to relate sounds to letters in phonics. Many cases of articulation defects clear up spontaneously by the age of seven or eight.

Auditory perception needs to be considered as well as auditory acuity. Here one is concerned with the intelligent interpretation of the sound waves picked up by the ears. Test measurements of auditory perception of elements of speech known to be critical for learning to read are highly correlated with later reading achievement (67, 92). Often called "auditory discrimination tests," these instruments may require children to decide which picture shows something that begins with the same sound as another pictured object. Or these tests may involve matching final rhymes or medial sounds.

If children are going to benefit from phonic instruction, they must be able to hear the sounds associated with the letters of the alphabet. It is clear also that most children entering kindergarten have ears fully equipped to hear these speech sounds. Shvatchkin (84) showed that by age two children already distinguish words that differ from one another by only a single phoneme (the unit of speech taught as "a sound" in phonics). Also, long before they come to kindergarten, children can use the phoneme patterns of the language in their own speech. However, Elkonin's studies (30) indicate that children at this preschool age level are not actually analyzing speech into these units of sound, and they are not aware that spoken language can be segmented into such elements. Several other studies show that the typical kindergarten beginner does not perceive speech as broken into units like the word or the phoneme (19, 20, 22, 35, 78).

These research results are not surprising when one considers that the preschooler's experience of language is of rapid, continuous speech in no way broken up into the segments represented in the printed code. These segments are arbitrary abstract concepts that were first thought of when visible language written with an alphabet was invented by our ancestors. Similarly, children first begin to think about these abstract ideas when they are given the tasks involved in learning to read. Thus, perception of the sound units of language has its fundamental basis in conceptual learning.

Conceptual Learning and Reasoning

Recent research reveals that the most important aspect of learning to read is the cognitive process. By this is meant the development of relevant *knowledge* about spoken and written language.

Fitts and Posner (*33*) reviewed all the research on skill development and concluded that all skill learning begins with a cognitive phase. This cognitive phase consists of the learners' efforts to figure out what they are supposed to learn and why. Vernon's first review of research on the causes of reading disability led her to conclude that "the fundamental and basic characteristic of reading disability appears to be cognitive confusion and lack of system" (*95*:71). She points out that cognitive confusion is the normal state of young school beginners. Thus, normal children work their ways out of this confusion into a state of *cognitive clarity*. They use their reasoning processes to figure out what they must do in reading and relate this process to its various purposes. In her latest review of research on reading difficulties, Vernon concludes that "in learning to read it is essential for the child to realize and understand" the fundamental principle of how the alphabet is used to code language experienced as speech prior to coming to school. Vernon emphasizes that "a thorough grasp of this principle necessitates a fairly advanced stage of conceptual reasoning..." (*96*:79)—thus establishing children's reasoning processes as key factors in learning to read.

In order to be able to reason about the reading process children must develop certain basic concepts about language: functional concepts and featural concepts. Downing reviewed the whole of the relevant research in detail in another book (*21*). The following discussion focuses on the main conclusions of importance for practical work in kindergarten and grade one.

Functional Concepts

The inventors of written language had to discover ideas about the communication purposes of language. With these concepts they designed written symbols for various communication purposes. These concepts of the purpose of written language have to be rediscovered by each child; they are learned from experience. Two studies by Downing, Ollila, and Oliver (*23, 24*) demonstrate this fact. Children from homes where parents were more likely to engage in literacy activities, such as reading and writing, had significantly clearer comprehension of the purposes of written language than children from homes where literacy behavior was less likely to be in evidence. Several studies show that children whose parents read to them have a head start in reading readiness (5) because these youngsters learn about purpose by sharing reading with someone who knows its value. The language experience approach in early reading provides many opportunities to learn the purposes of reading and writing because, from the very beginning, children use written language purposefully. The British Government's recent commission on reading instruction advocated only one specific method—the language experience approach. This 1975 Department of Education and Science report states: "Language development . . . involves creating situations in which, to satisfy his own purposes, a child encounters the need to use more elaborate forms and is thus motivated to extend the complexity of language available to him" (17:67). The report also warns that "Competence in language comes above all through its purposeful use, not through the working of exercises divorced from context" (p. 528).

David Russell wrote: "The dominant factor in comprehension, accordingly, is the purpose of the reader, stated or unstated" (79:170). Russell also concluded that "one of the most important reading heights is that of flexibility of reading in different ways for different purposes" (p. 152). That flexibility for differing reading purposes has its seed in children's first encounters with written language and the tasks they are given in the name of reading. From these early experiences of reading, children develop those essential concepts about the purposes of reading and writing.

Featural Concepts

The other equally important set of prerequisite concepts for reasoning about the reading process consists in abstract ideas on elements of spoken and written language, such as *word, sound, letter*, or *sentence*. Readers can imagine how cognitively confused they would be if their teachers said: "I'm going to *tove* some *bizzirs*. See these *bizzirs*. Their names are *snow* and *oog*. They say *hger*. Who knows a *klung* with the *movement* 'hger' in it?" One can translate these nonsense words into real words: "I'm going to *write* some *letters*. See these *letters*. Their names are *sea* and *aitch*. They say 'hger' (as in the Scottish *loch*). Who knows a *word* with the *sound* 'hger' in it?" Young children have nothing to reconstruct. They do not know the concepts to which these technical labels refer. These technical terms used in reading instruction are part of what DeStefano (18) calls "the language instruction register"—the special teaching terms used to talk about language. Children must learn the meanings of these terms in order to comprehend the teacher's instructions. But it is not so much the terms themselves that are important. As Piaget pointed out, in the normal course of development, "Verbal forms always evolve more slowly than actual understanding" (75:203). When children discover a concept they need a name for it.

Recent research shows that the normal young school beginner of kindergarten age does not possess such concepts as "a word," "a sound" (phoneme), "a letter," or "a sentence" (12, 19, 20, 22, 35, 49, 62, 78, 94). In her study, Francis found that "the children had never thought to analyze speech, but in learning to read had been forced to recognize units and subdivisions. The use of words like *letter, word,* and *sentence* in teaching was not so much a direct aid to instruction but a challenge to find their meaning." This is why Nila Banton Smith (87) concluded that "teachers should be made aware that simply teaching the names of the letters of the alphabet appears to be without value insofar as the task of learning to read is concerned." A name for something not understood is useless.

It seems obvious that children will comprehend their reading instruction more clearly if they understand the concepts the teacher is talking about. Thus a very important aspect of reading readiness is the understanding of these abstract concepts of the features of language that must be reasoned about in comprehending the reading process. What featural concepts are necessary depend on the teacher's methods of instruction. For example, if the teacher wants to teach phonics, the children will need to know what is meant by "a letter" and "a sound" (phoneme). As was shown earlier in this chapter in the section on "The ears and auditory perception," most kindergarten children have no difficulties in auditory discrimination. They are perfectly able to hear the difference between *cat* and *cats*. What they lack is the knowledge that *cat* has three phonemes but *cats* has four. They have not yet developed what Mattingly (61) calls "linguistic awareness."

Research in linguistics shows that the phoneme has no concrete reality in objective acoustic measurements of speech (57). For example, it is impossible to cut a tape recording of a person's speech so as to recognize individual phonemes. The sounds "heard" in phonic instruction are abstractions. Each phoneme is a category of many variations of speech sound. The discovery of the concept of the phoneme by the inventors of alphabets was a brilliant stroke of abstract reasoning. The same high level of abstract reasoning development is required from the young beginner to comprehend the teacher's instruction in phonics.

Research at the Haskins Laboratories shows that there are two stages in the development of this linguistic awareness. The first is the

Downing and Lundsteen

growth of *tacit knowledge*. This level is described as being typical of the normal beginner in kindergarten. But in order to comprehend phonics instruction the child needs *explicit knowledge*. Shankweiler and Liberman state that tacit knowledge "is sufficient, of course, for comprehension of the spoken message. Writing and reading on the other hand, demand an additional analytic capability. Even before the advent of writing, those who used speech poetically must have been able to count syllables in order to form the meter and to be aware of the phonemic level in order to make rhymes. Some such explicit knowledge of these properties of speech is a precondition for understanding the alphabetic principle" (81:308).

In another book, Downing (21) described some of the methods for helping children to develop this level of explicit knowledge in linguistic awareness. Various games and exercises have been developed in several countries (30, 70), but many more creative teaching ideas are needed to turn these research findings to good use in kindergarten and grade one classrooms. Also, new ideas are needed for reading readiness tests based on these research results. The first attempt to produce such a test was made by Evanechko, Ollila, Downing, and Braun (31). That test has been revised and is undergoing reliability and validity testing (2).

Other Factors in Reading Readiness

There are other psychological factors in reading readiness but most of them are of lesser importance than those described previously—visual perception, auditory perception, and conceptual learning and reasoning. One of these other factors is especially important, however, and may even swamp the three described thus far. This fourth factor is affect—emotion and motivation.

Figure II-1 is a map of the child's psychological situation in beginning to learn to read in early childhood. The perceptual and reasoning processes of the child are at the center. These are the child's tools for interpreting input from the teacher's reading instruction. The student tries to figure out the instruction on the basis of the other input source—the child's bank of past experiences of spoken language. The third source of input consists of other factors, especially the affective variable (emotion and motivation). These other factors may inhibit or facilitate the central perceptual and reasoning processes.

The important left-hand box in the diagram will be discussed further in later sections of this chapter which are devoted to an account of children's oral language development—another extremely important factor in children's readiness for learning to read. This present section focuses on the relationships between these three sources of input and children's perceptual and reasoning processes and gives special

Figure II-1

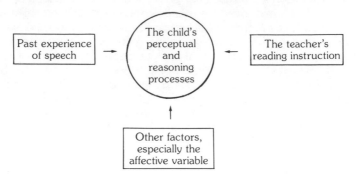

The Child's Psychological Situation in Beginning Reading

attention to other inhibiting or facilitating factors indicated by the lower box in figure II-1.

Most of these factors are derived from children's interactions with their environments. In the past, some theorists have argued that innate or inherited individual differences in children determine their level of readiness to learn to read. However, Downing and Thackray found in their review of the research that "there is little evidence to support the view that general maturity is an important factor in readiness to read" (26:17). They concluded that "the classroom teacher who wishes to judge a child's readiness for reading can obtain no practical help from a consideration of possible neurological factors as evidenced by such tendencies as crossed laterality, or reversals" (p. 30). Intelligence tests do correlate quite highly with reading achievement, but it is known now that these intelligence tests are strongly influenced by such environmental factors as poverty and membership in minority groups.

Similarly, the affective variable (emotion and motivation) gains most of its important strength from environmental influences. Even those psychiatric cases where emotional disturbance inhibits learning to read arise mostly from personality problems in family relationships. Much more common are cases where emotional disturbance has been caused by failure in learning to read. Gates' study (38) remains the definitive one on this point. He concluded that approximately 75 percent of the more severe cases of reading disability referred to clinics showed some degree of emotional disturbance. In one-quarter of these cases, the disturbance did cause the reading failure. But in three-quarters of the cases the emotional disturbance was the accompaniment or result of reading failure.

Gates (39) also demonstrated the significance of the other type of affective variable—motivation. In an experiment, individual children who had had no previous experience of learning to read were each presented with five boxes. Each box had one of five words on its top: *ball, bolt, bell, fall, roll.* The children were told that, if they could remember the word *ball* and open the box three times and find the real ball inside, they could keep it. All of the children started the game enthusiastically. Some were immediately successful and went on easily to more reading games. But other children were unable to master the task and became discouraged. As some of these children failed repeatedly, their interests faded and some showed evidence of disgust with the game. Gates' experiment shows how negative motivation can arise from tasks too difficult for beginners. Such attitudes could result in permanent dislike for reading that could inhibit perceptual and reasoning factors.

Motivation arises from many indirect influences in the environment, too. Space permits only two examples to be given here, but these motivational forces in the environment are many and they are often powerful.

One example serves to warn us against popular assumptions about innate differences among individual children. It is often claimed by North American theorists, and believed by many North American teachers and parents, that girls are innately superior to boys in language development in preschool and primary years. As a matter of fact, almost all the evidence from American reading research shows that, on an average, girls are more ready to learn to read than boys and that girls make better progress in reading in the primary grades (29). But if the American girls' superiority over the boys is due to biological differences in the sexes, others have pointed out that boys are superior in Germany (77), India (72), and Nigeria (1, 48). These sex differences in reading seem to be due to cultural-motivational factors. Recent research (27) showed that adults (teachers and nonteachers) in one North American city believed more often that reading is a feminine rather than a masculine activity. These beliefs were also reflected in the attitudes of the children in the same community. Another recent study (25) found that beliefs about the sex appropriateness of reading vary from one country to another. In all the countries studied, young boys began by accepting reading as a masculine activity. While American boys quickly learned to view reading as feminine, this was not the case in some other countries. In Denmark and Japan, for example, boys continued to believe that reading was appropriate for males. These studies of sex-role attitudes illustrate how cultural forces in the environment can give positive (American girls) or negative (American boys) motivation that may either facilitate or inhibit the perceptual and reasoning processes in learning to read.

Bilingual problems are discussed more fully later in this chapter; but here one may briefly mention the important motivational variable in attempts to overcome these language difficulties. Österberg (73) provided an experimental group of children in Piteå in the north of Sweden with beginning reading materials in their own nonstandard dialect of Swedish. A control group used the same readers in standard Swedish. The experimental group made more rapid progress in their nonstandard dialect materials than did the control group with the standard Swedish materials. Later the nonstandard dialect group overtook the standard group in their performance in reading standard Swedish. Referring to Figure II-1, the reason for this is clear. The young children in the experimental group could understand their reading instruction in their own dialect because they could relate it more clearly to their own past experiences of speech. On the other hand, the control group children's cognitive confusion was increased by instruction in a dialect (the standard dialect) they did not know. The experimental group of children who began reading in the nonstandard dialect gained greater cognitive clarity about the reading process because the nonstandard dialect materials and instruction fitted their own past experiences of speech. Consequently, the task of reasoning about the relationships between spoken and written language was simplified for them. Most important of all, these children could then apply their superior cognitive clarity to understanding written standard Swedish. Motivational forces favored this experimental group because the Piteå people are positive toward their own ancestral dialect.

In contrast, Stewart's attempt (89) to carry out a similar experiment with American Black English dialect in Washington, D.C., was wrecked by the cultural motivation factor. His experiment collapsed because of the "self-hate" of their own dialect displayed by the leaders in this minority group. They believed that the dialect materials were teaching "bad language" to their children.

These two contrasting experiments of Österberg and Stewart demonstrate the very great power of the affective variable. Perceptual and reasoning factors may be swamped by emotional or motivational forces. Nevertheless, the heart of the problem is one of perception and reasoning because that is the inherent nature of the task of learning to read. These studies of the affective variable in reading readiness indicate the basic perceptual and reasoning processes may either be helped or hindered by emotion or motivation. These processes also need a rich bank of previous experiences of language—our next topic.

The Child's Oral Language

Most educators are aware that there is a connection between children's maturity in speech development and their degree of success

Downing and Lundsteen

in learning to read. But often educators are not clear as to why and how oral language development should influence the acquisition of reading skill. On the one hand, early language development and beginning reading have some elements in common, serving the same purpose— communication. Both use language symbols, one using small visible black scratches on a page and the other using audible speech sounds in the air. There are similarities between meaning and kinds of sentences; both draw on a common background of feelings, experiences, concepts, and thinking strategies. If Marie cannot understand a line of discourse when it is read to her or when she tries to speak it, the chances are that she will not be able to read it either. The language may create a general problem for comprehension.

Although there are similarities between learning to speak one's mother tongue and learning to read, these two language skills differ in several important ways (59). For example, beginning reading instruction is usually relatively sudden in comparison with parental aid for learning to talk. Also, learning to talk is more immediately useful to the child than learning to read or write. It is important to recognize the intrinsic rewards stemming from social interaction in the course of learning spoken language. Often the motivating social element is missing in beginning reading. Indeed, it unfortunately sometimes carries instead punitive correction of errors. Another comparison is the amount of unnatural control and breaking apart of language associated with much beginning reading instruction.

Furthermore, the overall design of printed language itself is quite different in many ways from the oral speech to which children are accustomed. One of these differences is that individuals use speech and print for different purposes at various times, print generally being for more formal purposes. Also, speech and print make different demands on memory. A plus for print is that a reader can attend to several words at a time, select what those words will be, the order in which they will be dealt with, and the amount of time spent on them. Speech, however, usually has an advantage over reading because of the immediate, real life context in which it occurs. Its redundancy and the nonverbal accompaniments such as gestures help listeners to make intelligent guesses about the meaning that they can check as they go along. If children assume that they can make sense out of printed language in exactly the same way that they have made sense out of spoken language, they are likely to encounter difficulties (86). Children need help in seeing that book language and everyday language are not exactly the same.

These comparisons between written and oral language and the manner in which they are learned indicate some important principles for early reading instruction. First, one needs to keep in mind that the background needed for reading begins at birth. This developmental process must be continued by building upon perceptual, cognitive, linguistic, psychomotor, and communicative foundations. Children's experiences in art, music, drama, and literature should be maintained as foundations that have brought their development thus far (99). Children still need these ways of responding to lead them into the purposeful and creative use of written language. Second, the language that children are learning to read must be kept meaningful so they can make reasonable predictions about it on the basis of their past experiences of meaningful oral language.

In order to make decisions about children's reading programs, one needs to consider some important research facts about young children's memory processes, which are different from those of older children or adults. Memory is a special case of intelligent activity applied to recall and reconstruction of the past. It is not automatic and mindless (64). Young children, who are relatively less adept at remembering, need experience and familiarity with the type of information to be remembered (63). Children remember better if the information and its context are familiar, meaningful, and contain some internal organization (44). Finally, if young children are interested in and pay attention to information, they will remember it better. Being confronted with language of the *fat cat sat on the mat* variety bores most children, overloads their memory capacities, robs them of opportunities to organize their experiences for prediction, and thus makes learning to read more difficult. It should be mentioned also that, in teaching reading to children and particularly to those speaking nonstandard English, comprehension is much more important than standard English phonics (42, 87).

One reading method that fits in with the research described thus far is the language experience approach to reading (described in another chapter of this book). The material used in this method is developed by writing out the child's own experience as the youngster dictates it. The research mentioned above also suggests that the language experience approach needs to be accompanied by much reading aloud from good children's literature. Artistic books published for children give them the necessary exposure to the domain of printed language structures toward which children will continue to grow which youngsters will use with more and more flexibility and expertise. Literature in the program also serves children as truly motivating communication—a good reason to learn to read (11, 14, 15).

Children need ample opportunity to play and to talk with one another and with adults. Oral language development, the foundation of reading and writing, calls for talking and listening. Children are unlikely to read better than they can speak and listen. Oral language

Downing and Lundsteen

development is far from complete when children start school (10). Methods and approaches for insuring that this highly important development is fostered in school are described elsewhere in this book. Research sources administrators may find helpful are those by Garvey and Hogan (37), Labov (53), Mueller (65), and Lundsteen (58, 59).

Language Development of the Child

Individual children vary greatly in linguistic maturity, and it is important for school administrators and teachers to perceive beginning reading in its place in the time scale of overall language growth.

The child's process of learning the language of others develops in three stages: prelinguistic, protolinguistic, and true linguistic. The stages of cognitive development were outlined by Piaget (76) and Charles (9). These stages of language development correspond roughly to certain ages but with great individual variation. For example, Jean at age two can (rather precociously) name all the objects in her environment; Jim at age five (a perfectly normal child) still cannot. The point is that while the order of linguistic stages to follow is relatively stable, ages are merely approximate (4, 8, 16, 54, 56).

The first two stages usually occur long before school begins. Therefore, they need be mentioned here only briefly.

The *prelinguistic stage* comprises two subperiods: 1) birth to three months (gurgling and cooing) and 2) three to twelve months (babbling).

The *protolinguistic stage* usually occurs from twelve months to two years and is sometimes referred to as the walk-talk stage.

The stage that is important for the purposes of this book is the *true linguistic stage*. From about two to six years of age, children progressively and rapidly increase their vocabularies. For example, at age two children typically have 200 to 300 word vocabularies. Some children are able to name all items in their environments. The joining of words into original sentences continues. ("Hi sock!" says a child who is unlikely to have copied that utterance from an adult.) Children develop what appears to be a rudimentary grammar with rule-governed language behavior (development of syntax). According to linguists, this grammar is genuinely constructed by the children. It does not occur in adult language, nor is it a mere random throwing together of words. Children pulling what they need autonomously from their environments are impelled to make sense of their world and accomplish wondrous feats.

Next, children start coping with elements such as time, the manner in which they do things (adverbs), and word order becomes tried and tested. Throughout this language development, the pacesetter is the child's cognitive growth. Children use language to express what they already know. Vygotsky (97), however, indicated from his research on development of language and thought that, before the age of two, language tends to run ahead of thought. Children mutter aloud and then think and act. Gradually children internalize this overt speech; they think first and then speak. As concept formation develops, young children may use the word "doggie" to refer to dog, cat, horse, cow, or any four-legged animal. Eventually, children refine ideas, learn adult categories, and pinpoint language use.

By age six, children have use of most of the simple grammatical structures and sounds characteristic of the dialects closest to them. On into the elementary school years, however, some complex structures with less easily determined referents are still being mastered; for example, "John promised Mary to go" or "John asked Bill what to do" (10, 11, 69). Typically, spoken communication units at age six are about six to seven words long. Almost two years earlier, children have been able to share a connected account of some recent experience. From age four, children can usually carry out a sequence of two simple directions. By age five, when the experiences and language are familiar, children will typically be holding conversations with others and their language is usually easily understood.

As their thoughts forge ahead of their ease and fluency of performance (as their competency is ahead of their performance), children may repeat phrases, words, or even parts of words. This repetition is quite normal; it enables children to gain control over language which is often a fleeting experience.

Vocabulary development is incomplete, of course, at age six; meanings are often still superficial and multiple meanings for the same word may not be known. Children typically enter first grade with vocabularies of approximately 3,000 words and gain about 1,000 words a year thereafter. Some children are still refining use of verb tenses, pronouns, and plural forms. At about age four, children may invent words to meet their needs (for example, "spit-get" for spaghetti). Or they may employ words they already know as amusing substitutions. For example, a child with cold hands called out that he wanted his "muffins" (mittens); he told a friend that his mother was calling at the back "scream" (screen) and wanted a "middle-aged" (middle-sized) piece of cake.

Children typically understand and use words concretely before they use them abstractly ("deep water" before "deep secret," or "on a block" before "on Saturday") (32). In A Hole Is to Dig (50), there is a delightful collection of preschool children's concrete definitions ("a nose is to blow," "hands are to hold"). Research indicates that children develop progressively in competency for handling abstract meanings for their vocabularies (58).

Downing and Lundsteen

Children in the true linguistic stage show increasing ability to use relationships. They understand prepositions of spatial relationships to their own bodies ("place the hoop above your head") before understanding relationships to other objects in space ("place the hoop above the toy cow"). At about three years of age children begin to use words that describe position ("on," "in," "over," "in front of," "beside"). If children can understand than an object is "in the corner," they are aware of angles; if they can put the object "on the second shelf," they are aware of sequential ordering; if they can place the object correctly "with the other toys," they are likely to be aware of classification of like objects. These relational words ("above," "in," "on," "with") are descriptive of children's perceptions of their world and its many connections.

Children's speech marks what is relevant in their environment and affects their thinking. Early childhood educators find that children who have little or no experience with words that qualify relationships have trouble thinking and performing with them. In other words, children cannot perform using relational vocabulary items if they lack the experience filled with contrasts to give them underlying competence. Certain environments can provide these contrasts.

Some early childhood programs have segments and materials designed to promote competence and performance with positional concepts. It is a gross error to drill on these relational words in isolation without the meaningful, contrastive context of experience. This kind of mistake applies to preschool oral language programs as well as early reading programs.

Teachers cannot assume that children understand a word simply because they comprehend it in one particular situation. A word is not fully understood until children have sorted out the features distinguishing it from similar words and can understand the word's meaning in a full range of applicable situations. For example, the cognitive code vocabulary of many preschool programs includes words describing color and shape words such as more/less, big/bigger/biggest, small/smaller/smallest, between, behind, on top of, beside, and before/after (46). But these cognitive, code words are difficult because children must attend to the words' unchanging features and relationships across many individual contexts. Children must learn that all sorts of objects can be blue and that a whole range of shades is called "blue." The message for teaching is to provide word encounters in a variety of natural, practical situations. Drilling children to hear or say a word in a single, repeated situation will not help them learn the full meaning of the word in the range of situations to which it applies. Actually, a good teacher provides experiences in each activity and in each portion of the day (for example, at clean-up time when children are to place materials in various relationships, "Put the round block in the cubicle over the long, flat blocks."). Young children need extended exposure to many words in a variety of contexts.

Research by Sinclair-deZwart (85) is relevant to the topic of language and concept attainment. This researcher found that children who were able to perform Piaget's tasks, such as the arrangement of sticks in serial order, and children who were able to "conserve" used comparative language ("The boy has *more than* the girl."). The term *conservation* refers to grasping the fact of sameness in spite of the visual evidence of difference. For instance, two identically sized balls of clay are considered still the same, even when one is kept in a ball and the other is rolled out into a long sausage. Sinclair-deZwart found that children unable to conserve used absolute terms instead ("the boy has a lot," "the girl has a little"). She found that verbal training leads children who are unable to perform conservation tasks to direct their attention to pertinent aspects of the problem, to focus dually on attributes (both on tallness and on width). But, verbal training does not necessarily bring about the ability to conserve. The author concludes that language is not the source of logic but is structured by logic.

In other words, trying to rush stages of intellectual growth results in empty verbalization. Children may be able to mouth the words, but language performance will outstrip underlying thought. Construction of necessary foundations of thought takes time (45). Language is an aid to thought but not a guarantee to thought. Just giving children language is like giving them two-wheeled bicycles when they can't reach the pedals.

In language development children need adults who are good listeners and good conversationalists. Adults become better listeners when they sit or stoop to meet children at eye level. In fact, trying to see things from the child's point of view ("How would this child be thinking about this?") is the key to helping children develop language and thought. In this way, one can be sure to use real-life situations of genuine interest to both teacher and child. Then the teacher becomes an interacting model of language behavior. In one study, preschoolers' speech reflected the teacher's after only a few weeks (88).

Overt Speech as an Aid to Children's Creativity

As mentioned earlier, young children may mumble a lot to themselves. This egocentric speech may be highly important to children engaged in work or play such as painting a picture, modeling in clay, composing a picture story. Such speech is not undesirable; it is normal and useful and may enhance development of thought, productivity, and self-control (13, 98, 43). Graves found seven year olds using this mode of speech to advantage as they wrote compositions

　　　　　　　　　　　　　　　　　　Downing and Lundsteen

and made pictures that often went ahead of the written composition. Children talk to themselves while they work because it is their natural way of improving thought and language.

Young children have problems in interactive communication when they fail to understand what they must say in order to provide the information the listener needs to know. They are so egocentric in their speaking that as they send the message they code it for themselves. They assume: "I know what it's all about, so my listener must know what it's all about, too." They make no effort to take into account the listener's point of view (34, 60), Non-egocentric communication skills can be developed during normal classroom activities as children explain ongoing activities to a child who has just joined the group. Or the teacher can invite the child to tell it to an aide, who can probe for information omitted—for example, "What else does it look like?" "What did you do next?" (74). Meaningful context, meaningful audiences, genuine need for communication—this kind of demand for comprehension readies the child for insisting upon meaning while reading and for writing comprehensibly. Situations must be created for children to formulate clear and complete verbal messages. If children have difficulty with this task, one should help by asking questions and by providing examples of messages that communicate (41).

Children learn grammar quite naturally by imitating the speech patterns of people they love and admire. Drilling adult grammatical forms into young children has little lasting value and may rob children of joy in language and of self-esteem necessary for further development (5, 88).

The acquisition of sound production is especially documented by research. Type and frequency of phoneme (sound) production increases with age (83). When they enter first grade, most children have control of sounds that characterize their dialects. Templin (91) discovered that, by age six, 75 percent of the youngsters she studied produced /t/, /th/ (as in thin, unvoiced) /v/, and /l/; by age seven, /th/ (as in then, voiced), /z/, /zh/, and /j/. In other words, by age six the only distinctive speech sounds not produced by at least 90 percent of the sample were /s/, /sh/ (as in mission), /z/, /zh/ (as in vision), /th/ (as in either), /ch/ (as in church) and /hw/ (as in why). In the primary grades, children are still growing in speech production and in speech reception (listening). A child's sound substitutions such as "wady" for "lady" and "tat" for "cat" may not mean inability to say correct sounds but failure to note the difference in sounds another person makes—inability to listen.

Unfortunately, some parents become concerned that their children may never make certain sounds correctly and prematurely bundle the youngsters off to speech therapists. Some teachers may spend long hours of their time and (worse yet) the children's time trying to teach speech sounds and letter correspondences that children are not yet ready to pronounce nor differentiate when listening.

Perhaps one of the most important things to remember about language stages emerging from the research is that they are not norms for which teachers and pupils must be held accountable. Normally, children vary greatly as to when they go through these stages. Some children do not even do the sorts of things suggested at each language stage. The progressive mastery outlined is not necessarily related to future language fluency and effectiveness for any one given individual. Children do go through stages in an apparently rather fixed order, but they show much variation as to "how."

Bilingual, Culturally Different, and Learning Disabled Children

Much of what we know about oral language and the typical child applies equally to the special child and to children who are economically disadvantaged or culturally different. Well-rationalized, developmental teaching helps almost all children. If a child is special, the teacher needs to know as much as possible about that child's specialness and particular social context.

What specific guidance does research offer for children who speak nonstandard English? Children who speak nonstandard English are not speaking a grammatically immature or deficient language. Children's grammar needs to be evaluated in terms of the native language or dialect they are acquiring (53, 16). For young children whose grammar reflects a developing form of nonstandard English, a strategy of acceptance and modeling is just as appropriate for children whose native dialect is standard English (7, 90).

There is no evidence that, as a whole, one language is better or more complex than any other language (55). Pressure to convert the grammar and pronunciation of young children who speak nonstandard English to standard English fails. Children can understand and read standard English without habitually speaking it. Nonstandard English is quite adequate as a tool for thinking and communicating (7, 51, 52). Some schools have tried language drill programs for these kinds of students. Apparent success may grow out of training children in teacher-pleasing skills and the presence of one-to-one contact that should be helpful to almost any child, especially if the teacher is enthusiastic (98). There is no reason to think that the success of language drill programs—learning a limited set of words and expressions in a rigid, repetitive format—improves children's thinking (46). On the contrary, research from child psychology and linguistics indicates that the surest way to succeed in this work is to know the children's culturally different backgrounds and languages, to know special children's unique problems and strengths, and then to create the environments where communications flourish in meaningful ways—no matter how young or how special or how different.

References

1. Abiri, J.O.O. "World Initial Teaching Alphabet versus Traditional Orthography," doctoral dissertation, University of Ibadan, Nigeria, 1969.
2. Ayers, D., J. Downing, and B. Schaefer. *Test of Linguistic Awareness in Reading Readiness.* Victoria, Canada: University of Victoria, 1977.
3. Bedwell, C.H. "The Significance of Visual, Ocular, and Postural Anomalies in Reading and Writing," in William Latham (Ed.), *The Road to Effective Reading.* London: Ward Lock, 1975.
4. Britton, J. *Language and Learning.* Coral Gables, Florida: University of Miami Press, 1970.
5. Brown, Roger. *A First Language.* Cambridge, Massachusetts: Harvard University Press, 1973.
6. Brzeinski, J.E. "Beginning Reading in Denver," *Reading Teacher,* 18 (1964), 16-21.
7. Burling, R. *English in Black and White.* New York: Holt, Rinehart and Winston, 1973.
8. Cazden, C.B. *Child Language and Education.* New York: Holt, Rinehart and Winston, 1972.
9. Charles, C.M. *Teacher's Petit Piaget.* Belmont, California: Fearon, 1974.
10. Chomsky, C. *The Acquisition of Syntax in Children from Five to Ten.* Cambridge, Massachusetts: MIT Press, 1969.
11. Chomsky, C. "Stages in Language Development and Reading Exposure," *Harvard Educational Review,* 42 (1972), 1-33.
12. Clay, M.M. *Reading: The Patterning of Complex Behaviour.* Auckland, New Zealand: Heinemann, 1962.
13. Conrad, R. "The Chronology of the Development of Cover Speech in Children," *Developmental Psychology,* 5 (1971), 398-405.
14. Cullinan, B.E., A.M. Jagger, and D. Strickland. "Language Expansion for Black Children in the Primary Grades: A Research Report," *Young Children,* 30 (1974), 98-111.
15. Cullinan, B.E., and C.W. Carmichael (Eds.). *Literature and Young Children.* Urbana, Illinois: National Council of Teachers of English, 1977.
16. Dale, P.S. *Language Development: Structure and Function.* Hinsdale, Illinois: Dryden Press, 1972.
17. Department of Education and Science. *A Language for Life* (The Bullock Report). London: Her Majesty's Stationery Office, 1975.
18. De Stefano, J.S. *Some Parameters of Register in Adult and Child Speech.* Louvain, Belgium: Institute of Applied Linguistics, 1972.
19. Downing, J. "Children's Concepts of Language in Learning to Read," *Educational Research,* 12 (1970), 106-112.
20. Downing, J. "Children's Developing Concepts of Spoken and Written Language," *Journal of Reading Behaviour,* 4 (1972), 1-19.
21. Downing, J. *Reading and Reasoning.* Edinburgh: Chambers, 1979.
22. Downing, J., and P. Oliver. "The Child's Concept of 'a Word," *Reading Research Quarterly,* 9 (1974), 568-582.
23. Downing, J., L. Ollila, and P. Oliver. "Cultural Differences in Children's Concepts of Reading and Writing," *British Journal of Educational Psychology,* 45 (1975), 312-316.

24. Downing, J., L. Ollila, and P. Oliver. "Concepts of Language in Children from Differing Socioeconomic Backgrounds," *Journal of Educational Research*, 70 (1977), 277-281.

25. Downing, J., and others. *A Cross-National Survey of Cultural Expectations and Sex-Role Standards in Reading*, 1978.

26. Downing, J., and D.V. Thackray. *Reading Readiness*, Second Edition. London: Hodder and Stoughton, 1975.

27. Downing, J., and D. Thomson. "Sex-Role Stereotypes in Learning to Read," *Research in the Teaching of English*, 1977.

28. Durrell, D.D. *Improving Reading Instruction*. New York: World Book, 1956.

29. Dykstra, R., and R. Tinney. "Sex Differences in Reading Readiness—First Grade Achievement and Second Grade Achievement," in J.A. Figurel (Ed.), *Reading and Realism*. Newark, Delaware: International Reading Association, 1969.

30. Elkonin, D.B. "U.S.S.R." in John Downing (Ed.), *Comparative Reading*. New York: Macmillan, 1973.

31. Evanechko, P., and others. "An Investigation of the Reading Readiness Domain," *Research in the Teaching of Reading*, 7 (1973), 61-78.

32. Feofanov, M.P. "On the Use of Prepositions in a Child's Speech," *Voprosy Psikhol*, 3 (1959), 118-124.

33. Fitts, P.M., and M.I. Posner. *Human Performance*. Belmont, California: Brooks-Cole, 1967.

34. Flavel, J.H. "Role-Taking and Communication Skills in Children," in W.W. Hartup and N.L. Smothergill (Eds.), *The Young Child*. Washington, D.C.: National Association for the Education of Young Children, 59-76, 1967.

35. Francis, H. "Children's Experiences of Reading and Notions of Units in Language," *British Journal of Educational Psychology*, 43 (1973), 17-23.

36. Frostig, M. "Visual Modality and Reading," in H.K. Smith (Ed.), *Perception and Reading*. Newark, Delaware: International Reading Association, 1968.

37. Garvey, C., and R. Hogan. "Social Speech and Social Interaction: Egocentrism Revisited," *Child Development*, 44 (1973), 562-658.

38. Gates, A.I. "The Role of Personality Maladjustment in Reading Disability," *Journal of Genetic Psychology*, 59 (1941), 77-83.

39. Gates, A.I. *The Improvement of Reading*, Third Edition. New York: Macmillan, 1949.

40. Gavel, S.R. "June Reading Achievement of First Grade Children," *Journal of Education*, 140 (1958), 30-43.

41. Gleason, J.B. "An Experimental Approach to Improving Children's Communication Ability," in C. B. Cazden (Ed.), *Language in Early Childhood Education*. Washington, D.C.: National Association for the Education of Young Children, 1972.

42. Goodman, K.S., and Y.M. Goodman. "Learning about Psycholinguistic Processes by Analyzing Oral Reading," *Harvard Educational Review*, 77 (1977), 317-333.

43. Graves, D.R. "Children's Writing: Research Directions and Hypotheses Based upon an Examination of the Writing Processes of Seven Year Old Children," doctoral dissertation, State University of New York at Buffalo, 1973. *Dissertation Abstracts International*, 34 (1974), 6255A. University Microfilms No. 74-08375. ED 095 586.

44. Hall, J.W., and M.S. Halperin. "The Development of Memory-Encoding Processes in Young Children," *Developmental Psychology*, 6 (1972), 181.

45. Inhelder, B. "Information Processing Tendencies in Recent Experiments in Cognitive Learning—Empirical Studies," in Sylvia Farmhan-Diggory (Ed.), *Information Processing in Children*. New York: Academic Press, 1972.

46. Jackson, Nancy E., Halbert B. Robinson, and Philip S. Dale. *Cognitive Development in Young Children: A Report for Teachers*. Washington, D.C.: U. S. Department of Health Education and Welfare, National Institute of Education, 1976.

47. Jacobs, J., and others. "A Follow-Up Evaluation of the Frostig Visual-Perceptual Training Program," *Educational Leadership*, 26 (1968), 169-175.
48. Johnson, D.D. "Sex Differences in Reading Across Cultures," *Reading Research Quarterly*, 9 (1973-1974), 67-86.
49. Kingston, A.J., W.W. Weaver, and L.E. Figa. "Experiments in Children's Perception of Words and Word Boundaries," in Frank P. Greene (Ed.), *Investigations Related to Mature Reading*. Milwaukee, Wisconsin: National Reading Conference, 1972.
50. Kraun, R. *A Hole Is to Dig*. New York: Harper and Row, 1952.
51. Labov, W. "Some Sources of Reading Problems for Negro Speakers of Nonstandard English," in J.S. Baratz and R. W. Shuy (Eds.), *Teaching Black Children to Read*. Washington, D.C.: Center for Applied Linguistics, 1969.
52. Labov, W. *The Study of Nonstandard English*. Urbana, Illinois: National Council of Teachers of English, 1970.
53. Labov, W. *Language in the Inner City*. Philadelphia: University of Pennsylvania, 1972.
54. Landreth, C. *Early Childhood: Behaviour and Learning*. New York: Knopf, 1967.
55. Langacker, R.W. *Language and Its Structure*. New York: Harcourt Brace Jovanovich, 1973.
56. Lenneberg, E.H. *Biological Foundations of Language*. New York: Wiley, 1967.
57. Liberman, A.M., and others. "Perception of the Speech Code," *Psychological Review*, 74 (1967), 431-461.
58. Lundsteen, S.W. *Children Learn to Communicate*. Englewood Cliffs, New Jersey: Prentice-Hall, 1976.
59. Lundsteen, S.W. "On Developmental Relations between Language-Learning and Reading," *Elementary School Journal*, 77 (1977), 192-203.
60. Maratsos, M.P. "Nonegocentric Communication Abilities in Preschool Children," *Child Development*, 44 (1973), 747-752.
61. Mattingly, I.G. "Reading, the Linguistic Process, and Linguistic Awareness," in J.F. Kavanagh and I.G. Mattingly (Eds.), *Language by Ear and by Eye*. Cambridge, Massachusetts: MIT Press, 1972.
62. Meltzer, N.S., and R. Herse. "The Boundaries of Written Words as Seen by First Graders," *Journal of Reading Behavior*, 1 (1969), 3-14.
63. Milgram, N.A., M.F. Shore, and C. Malasky. "Linguistic and Thematic Variables in Recall of a Story by Disadvantaged Children," *Child Development*, 42 (1971), 637-640.
64. Morin, R.E., K.L. Hoving, and D.S. Konick. "Short-Term Memory in Children: Keeping Track of Variables with Few or Many States," *Journal of Experimental Child Psychology, 10 (1970), 181-188.*
65. Mueller, E. "The Maintenance of Verbal Exchanges between Young Children," *Child Development*, 43 (1972), 930-938.
66. Nicholson, A. "Background Abilities Related to Reading Success in First Grade," *Journal of Education*, 140 (1958), 7-24.
67. Nila, Sr. M. "An Experimental Study of Progress in First Grade Reading," *Catholic University of America Educational Research Bulletin*, 4 (1940), 48.
68. Ollila, L. "The Effects of Three Contrasting Readiness Programs on the Readiness Skill of Kindergarten Boys and Girls," doctoral dissertation, University of Minnesota, 1970.
69. Ollila, L., and L. Chamberlain. "The Learning and Retention of Two Classes of Graphic Words: High Frequency Nouns and Non-Noun Words among Kindergarten Children," *Journal of Educational Research*, 72 (1979), 288-293.
70. Ollila, L., T. Johnson, and J. Downing. "Adapting Russian Methods of Auditory Discrimination Training," *Elementary English*, 51 (1974), 1138-1141, 1145.
71. Olson, A.V. "Growth in Word Perception Ability as it Relates to Success in Begin-

ning Reading," *Journal of Education*, 140 (1958), 25-36.

72. Oommen, C. "India," in John Downing (Ed.), *Comparative Reading*. New York: Macmillan, 1973.

73. Österberg, T. *Bilingualism and the First School Language*. Umea, Sweden: Vasterbottens Tryekeri, AB, 1961.

74. Peterson, C.L., F. W. Danner, and J.H. Flavell. "Developmental Changes in Children's Response to Three Indications of Communicative Failure," *Child Development*, 43 (1972), 1463-1468.

75. Piaget, J. *The Language and Thought of the Child*, Third Edition. London: Routledge and Kegan Paul, 1959.

76. Piaget, J. "The Theory of Stages in Cognitive Development," address presented at the CTB/McGraw-Hill Invitational Conference on Ordinal Scales of Cognitive Development, Monterey, California, February 1969.

77. Preston, R.C. "Reading Achievement of German and American Children," *School and Society*, 90 (1962), 350-354.

78. Reid, J.F. "Learning to Think about Reading," *Educational Research*, 9 (1966), 56-62.

79. Russell, D.H. *The Dynamics of Reading*. Waltham, Massachusetts: Ginn-Blaisdell, 1970.

80. Samuels, S.J. "Letter-Name versus Letter-Sound Knowledge in Learning to Read," *Reading Teacher*, 24 (1971), 604-608.

81. Shankweiler, D., and I.Y. Liberman. "Exploring the Relations between Reading and Speech," in R.M. Knights and D.J. Baker (Eds.), *Neuropsychology of Learning Disorders: Theoretical Approaches*. Baltimore: University Park Press, 1976.

82. Shaw, J.H. "Vison and Seeing Skills of Preschool Children," *Reading Teacher*, 18 (1964), 33-36.

83. Shuy, Roger. "What Teachers Should Know about the Language of Children," paper presented at the Fifth Annual National Conference on the Language Arts in the Elementary School, National Council of Teachers of English, Chicago, 1973.

84. Shvatchkin, N.Kh. "The Development of Phonematic Perception of Speech in Young Children," *News of the Academy of Psychological Science of the Russian Soviet Federative Socialist Republic*, 1948, 13.

85. Sinclair-deZwart, H. "Developmental Psycholinguistics," in D. Elkind and J.J. Flavel (Eds.), *Studies in Cognitive Development: Essays in Honor of Jean Piaget*. New York: Oxford University Press, 1969.

86. Smith, F. "Making Sense of Reading—and of Reading Instruction," *Harvard Educational Review*, 47 (1977), 386-395.

87. Smith, N.B. "Reading Research: Some Notable Findings," *Elementary English*, 50 (1972), 259-263, 269.

88. Smothergill, N.L., F. Olson, and S.G. Moore. "The Effects of Manipulation of Teacher Communication Style in the Preschool," *Child Development*, 42 (1971), 1227-1239.

89. Stewart, W.A. "Teaching Blacks to Read against Their Will," in P.A. Luelsdorff (Ed.), *Linguistic Perspectives on Black English*. Regensburg, Germany: Verlag Hans Carl, 1975.

90. Strickland, D.S. "A Program for Linguistically Different Black Children," *Research in the Teaching of English*, 7 (1973), 79-86.

91. Templin, M.C. *Certain Language Skills in Children: Their Development and Interrelationships*. Minneapolis: University of Minnesota Press, 1957.

92. Thackray, D.V. *Readiness to Read with i.t.a. and t.o.* London: Geoffrey Chapman, 1971.

93. Tronick, E.D., H. Als, and T.B. Brazelton. "Mutuality in Mother-Infant Interaction," *Journal of Communication*, 27 (1977), 74-79.

94. Turnbull, K. "Children's Thinking: When is a Letter a Number?" *Curriculum and Research Bulletin* (Victoria, Australia), 1970, 126-131.
95. Vernon, M.D. *Backwardness in Reading*. London: Cambridge University Press, 1957.
96. Vernon, M.D. *Reading and Its Difficulties*. London: Cambridge University Press, 1971.
97. Vygotsky, L. *Thought and Language*. Cambridge, Massachusetts: MIT Press, 1962.
98. White, S.H., and others. *Federal Programs for Young Children: Review and Recommendations*. Washington, D.C.: U.S. Government Publication No. OS 74-100, 1973.
99. Williams, R.M. "Why Children Should Draw," *Saturday Review*, September 3, 1977, 11-16.
100. Wingert, R.C. "Evaluation of a Readiness Training Program," *Reading Teacher*, 22 (1969), 325-329.
101. Wolff, P., J. Levin, and E.T. Longobardi. "Motoric Mediation in Children's Paired-Associate Learning: Effects of Visual and Tactual Contact," *Journal of Experimental Child Psychology*, 14 (1972), 176-183.

The Role of the Administrator 3

James H. Olson
James Childs
Jeanne Hammond

How Does a School Develop a Philosophy of Prereading Education?

Sunshine, raindrops, and individual differences. Individual differences do exist in kindergarten, just as they exist throughout the grades. Any attempt to teach reading or prereading skills in the kindergarten necessitates a departure from whole class instruction. The recognition of individual differences must form the base of any philosophy of prereading education. The administrator and staff must accept this premise and then go about the task of developing and extending each child's abilities.

The range of individual differences among kindergartners has truly broadened recently due to the effects of private nursery schools, preschools, day care centers, and *Sesame Street.* In a typical kindergarten, teachers (and administrators who are ultimately responsible) can expect to encounter children who possess language and reasoning skills similar to those of an average three year old, as well as children whose thinking, speaking, and reading skills are similar to the average seven to eight year old (*1:83*).

Uniqueness of Kindergarten

Every grade enjoys its own uniqueness due to the age range and maturity levels of the children and the content of the curriculum, a uniqueness most clearly exemplified in kindergarten. By age five, much of a child's capacity for learning has developed; however, children are quite malleable —age five is an important time for developing healthy attitudes toward school and learning in general. Because kindergarten is a child's first experience in a public school setting and for some children a first experience in a school setting of any kind, it is crucial that there be a smooth transition from dependence on home and family to a new independence and interaction with the school's authority figures, different rules, and large groups of peers. For these reasons, perhaps, more time is spent on orientation in kindergarten than in any other grade. Another unique feature of kindergarten is the opportunity afforded for play experiences. The kindergarten curriculum focuses on social, emotional, intellectual, and physical growth of the individual child, with equal consideration for each of these needs. Play experiences with peers provide excellent opportunities for growth in all of the goals of the kindergarten curriculum.

Curriculum Demands

Each year, kindergarten curriculum demands increase, as evidenced by a comparison of today's kindergarten curriculum with that of just ten years ago. In addition to formal reading programs, many kindergartens have established curriculums in arithmetic, science, social studies, language arts, and physical education. Whereas kindergarten was at one time primarily an informal setting with heavy emphasis on play situations and socialization skills, present day kindergarten schedules provide much less time for traditional activities. To some extent, curricular growth is justified, since the typical child of today seems more advanced in areas such as readiness skills, independence, and awareness of the world. However, the length of a kindergarten session is usually just two and one-half hours, making it extremely difficult to include both the expected curriculum and the needed orientation and play experience.

A typical kindergarten day might include the following:

Opening - attendance, pledge to the flag, song, calendar, weather chart (show and tell on Mondays and Wednesdays only).   10 minutes

Reading Readiness - in groups, utilizing centers for those not with a teacher. *Centers:* The class is divided into groups according to ability, leadership, and independence. Each group of four or five children works at a different center each day of the week for approximately 15 minutes, until all groups have visited five centers: 1) Creative, 2) Readiness, 3) Listening, 4) Task, and 5) Library. At several centers a choice of activities helps to provide for individual differences. During center time the children are expected to work independently, efficiently, and quietly.   20 minutes

Social Studies or Science   15 minutes

Worktime - usually art work pertaining to science or social studies unit.   15 minutes

Playtime - children have choice of activity. Teacher tries to see that it is varied each day so no child always plays with the same thing.   15 minutes

Language Arts	15 minutes
Physical Education - (twice a week) or *Library* (once a week).	25 minutes
Math	15 minutes
Music and Games	10 minutes
Evaluation of Day and Dismissal	5 minutes

Times for activities vary. For example, if physical education and library are not scheduled for a certain day, then other activities can be lengthened or combined, if appropriate.

Uniqueness May Bring about Isolation

Kindergarten teachers sometimes have a tendency to isolate themselves from other staff members. If there are only one or two kindergarten teachers in the school they can become busy and allow little time for socializing. They also could feel a need to protect or overemphasize their children's uniqueness. It is the administrator's responsibility to create opportunities for kindergarten teachers to interact with all members of the staff. The administrator could take a class; specialists in music, physical education, or art could be called in to help; or a substitute could be hired for a morning. Professional growth might be encouraged through flexible grade assignments, affording opportunities for kindergarten teachers to teach first or second grade, and vice versa. Obviously, it is vital to know and understand the characteristics of the age of the children in the grade one teaches as well as the curriculum expectations. However, it is also important to know where the children have come from and where they will be going in order to gain a wider perspective and deeper understanding of where they are at the moment. It is important for the kindergarten teacher to work closely with first grade teachers. Opportunities can be created for primary children and teachers to intermingle with kindergartners through activities such as *art exchange* (where children sign up for art projects without regard to grade level) or *mini-units* (where children sign up for areas of interest such as soccer, puppets, creative dramatics, and music). Similar numbers of primary grade children go to the kindergarten teacher for like activities. There also can be joint kindergarten-primary sing-a-longs or field trips. The important point here is that there is sometimes a tendency to develop a kindergarten reading program and policies apart from the total school program. It is the responsibility of the administrator to insure K-6 program development.

Professional Cooperation

One objective the administrator should keep in mind at all times is the importance of furthering staff cohesiveness, notably in the systematic teaching of reading. Frequent sessions with the administrator, reading specialist, kindergarten teacher, and primary teachers should help avoid problems, allow for policy formulation, and promote staff cohesiveness. As Singer observes, ". . . what makes for significant and cumulative improvement in the achievement of an entire elementary school is not each teacher having his or her own reading program, but a faculty committed to and experienced in a systematic, coherent reading program. Then, as each teacher makes a difference in the reading achievement of students, the result can be cumulative throughout the grades" (2:162-163). This is not to say that every child in kindergarten experiences reading instruction but that the kindergarten teacher is viewed as an integral part of the K-6 elementary reading program.

The philosophy of prereading education is, in so many respects, already there. The teacher must cherish the existence of individual differences and extend each child's abilities. The administrator must support the kindergarten teacher in any endeavor to provide for these individual differences. A staff and administrator may decide on *how* they will provide for individual differences and thus form a building-wide philosophy. Whether to teach reading in the kindergarten is no longer the issue, for individual differences demand the teaching of reading. The issues are: 1) to whom are reading and reading readiness skills to be taught and how? and 2) to whom are learning readiness and language skills to be taught and how?

How Will Resources be Allocated?

Financial Resources

Supplying the necessary equipment and materials for a kindergarten room is considerably different from providing the basic supplies needed at grade levels. Educational materials and large manipulative items are very expensive and yet need to be replaced periodically (e.g., a single large wooden truck costs $30 to $45). In addition to such regular expenditures for the standard kindergarten curriculum, there are presently special curriculum needs (reading workbooks, math workbooks, science and social studies kits, and games for reviewing concepts in all areas). For any early or prereading program to be successful, funding must be available for necessary materials. The administrator must understand that for the reading program to be successful, additional funds for materials over and above the standard kindergarten curriculum items must be available. Ordering becomes increasingly difficult since the prices of supplies have escalated 75 to 100 percent over the past ten years on items such as paper, paints, and paint brushes. The principal should ask the kindergarten teacher to work with the reading specialist in order to avoid overlap in ordering reading supplies and materials, particularly manipulative materials. Cooperation among different grade levels and curriculum specialists in sharing certain expensive items becomes necessary and can create opportunities for establishing rapport and understanding among kindergarten teachers, reading specialists, and the rest of the staff.

Personnel Resources

The administrator should make the kindergarten teachers a part of the total school effort by insisting that all kindergarten classes receive equal time from all support personnel, such as the music teachers, gym teachers, and reading teachers. Arranging for all resource people to work with kindergartners assures that more than one person works with each child. For too many years, kindergarten teachers have been the only professional persons making decisions about the children. Mainstreaming has certainly become a reality in the public schools. In the process of determining children's needs, the administrator must insure that the resource team is servicing kindergarten children. Moreover, kindergarten teachers must be integrally involved in whatever decisions are made about their students.

Another aspect of "use of resources" by the administrator has to do with class size. Somehow, despite all the voluminous research conducted on the teaching of reading, no one has satisfactorily dealt with class size. Too little research exists to guide educators. The profession needs to look beyond standardized test scores for the benefits derived from a reduced class size. The administrator must be aware of kindergartners' needs and abilities. Administrators (including central office personnel and the superintendent) need to spend time in kindergarten classrooms getting to know that the difference between twenty-two and thirty children in one classroom could be greater than eight!

What Must the Administrator Know about Teaching Reading?

Leadership

Ideally, every administrator should be an instructional leader who 1) has had recent teaching experience in K-6, 2) has credibility with the staff, 3) conducts an ongoing supervisory program of continually upgrading teacher competencies, and 4) demonstrates leadership within the school as well as in the community. In providing leadership in reading instruction, the administrator needs to employ sound practices of administration and supervision and seek the assistance of the building reading specialist or district reading consultant on matters of sound reading instruction. The administrator ought to be aware of the accepted practices or bases of the district's adopted reading program. These bases may differ from district to district because of a stated philosophy or program in use but should remain constant across a district. In one particular school system, for example, the district reading coordinator communicated to the elementary administrators the following "cornerstones" or bases of effective reading instruction:

1. A *single basal series*, accompanied by a wealth of integrally-related, commercial and/or teacher-made support material.
2. *Mastery* of skills, assessed through a criterion-referenced testing program.
3. Insurance for individual children's *success* through proper placement at each youngster's instructional reading level.
4. Adequate *time* devoted to reading instruction.
5. A structured and systematically taught program.
6. Small-group based instruction, with constant attention to differentiating instruction within those groups.
7. Emphasis on decoding words and understanding the meaning of what has been read.
8. Continuous progress (children pick up in fall where they left off previous spring).
9. Frequent assessment of progress.
10. Lessons made as multisensory as possible.
11. Attention to readiness concept (walking the tightrope between the need for success and the need to challenge).

Successful administrators continue to learn as much as they can about the reading process although they are not expected to be reading experts. In performing the following duties, administrators can also exercise leadership:

1. Develop staff awareness of the importance of reading and call their attention to articles on reading.
2. Use reading as one of the bases for division of classes for the succeeding year.
3. Require lesson plans; read them and ask questions.
4. Know where you can get help (i.e., district reading consultant or building reading specialist).
5. Know sound organizational practices.

6. Create opportunities for inservice training and encourage widespread participation.
7. Be comfortable, saying "I don't know, but I'll find out"; then, be sure to do so.
8. Be certain to have the immediate superior's support when insisting on adherence to the district curriculum.
9. Ask for help from and share positive experiences with other administrators in the district.
10. Insure that the total staff understands the reading program.
11. Use supervisory techniques such as having reading tests reviewed regularly by the reading specialist or having teachers list all reading groups and their instructional level periodically throughout the year.

Administrators must understand the time squeeze felt by kindergarten teachers in order to adequately team kindergarten teachers within a building or allocate the reading specialist's time in kindergarten. For example, the plan outlined below makes use of a kindergarten teacher and a reading teacher within the kindergarten class during reading time:

	Teacher X	Teacher Y	Centers
Day 1	Group A	Group B	Group C
Day 2	Group A	Group C	Group B
Day 3	Group B	Group C	Group A

Supervision

Observation through classroom visitation is the most important tool in insuring an effective reading program, and administrators should make classroom visits a priority. One useful technique is to arrange ten minute observations for particular skills several times during an entire week. Opportunities for supervision, developing understanding, and improving credibility can be gained if the administrator takes a reading group for a day or longer. Even going into a kindergarten classroom to read a story aloud is helpful. The benefits of visiting or substituting by the administrator are well worth the effort. Children love to see their principal in a role different from that of a disciplinary figure. Parents, children, and teachers need to be reminded that the administrator is first of all a teacher. The administrator and staff can work together to create opportunities for the administrator to become involved with children. For example, the principal could:

1. Assist with a special project or lesson requiring two adults.
2. Oversee a center where child guidance is needed.

Olson, Childs, and Hammond

3. Teach an already prepared lesson while the kindergarten teacher observes another teacher.
4. Teach a lesson while the kindergarten teacher tests individual children on reading skills.
5. Become involved in parent sharing sessions where the reading program is examined by parents and explained by teachers.

What Is the Administrator's Role in Relation to Other Personnel?

The administrator needs to make certain that the entire staff is aware of the reading curriculum. The building reading specialist or district consultant may provide expertise suggestions. The format for this information-sharing may be through periodic faculty meetings devoted to curricula or as part of a more intensive staff development program. A practice with which the writers have had considerable success is termed a "qualitative review." It is part of the overall reading evaluation plan of the district. In addition to standardized testing and criterion-referenced testing the reading evaluation committee felt that an added dimension of assessment should be a periodic discussion of questions such as those that follow (starred items have particular relevance for kindergarten):

1. *Grouping*
   *a. How many children per group? _____ Book? _____ Magazine? _____
   *b. How many minutes do you spend in reading per day?_____ What is the number of times that you meet each week with each group? _____
   *c. Is there a need to change a child to another group at this time? _____
2. *Mastery*
   Do you have any concerns with
   a. Criterion referenced testing? _____
   b. Reteaching? _____
   c. Retesting? _____
3. *Record Keeping*
   a. Are your records up to date? _____
   b. Do you have any clarification and procedure concerns? ___
4. *Materials*
   *a. What do you need in terms of the district reading program?
   *b. What support material do you need?
5. *Gifted Child*
   *a. How can we better meet the needs of the gifted children in your room?

6. *Pupils Having Difficulty within the District Program*
   a. Do you have any concerns with
      (1) Children new to the school?
      (2) Children presently in the series needing more exposure?
     *(3) Needs for supplementary short-term teaching reinforcement?
   b. Adjustment of the program to meet the needs of those children not successful in the district program at this time. Suggested steps for changing material would take into consideration the following:
      (1) Has the child been tested by the psychologist?
      (2) Has the reading teacher been involved?
      (3) Has the learning disabilities teacher been involved?
      (4) Has full use been made of the support materials?
      (5) What other program can be used?

The primary purpose of the *qualitative review* is to create a better informed administrator and staff and, hence, prevent problems before they became critical. The administrator's relationship and responsibility to other staff members, then, is one of interpretation and support. Everyone must know the goals and objectives of the reading program and the part each person plays. The major point the administrator must bear in mind is that there is only one supervisor in an elementary school—the principal. To put support personnel, such as reading teachers, in supervisory roles will ultimately destory those persons' rapport with the staff as well as place additional demands on them. The administrator must accept responsibility for all areas of direct supervision—financial, inservice, evaluation, record keeping, planning, and reporting to parents.

Recently, teaching staffs have grown to include additional resource persons such as learning disability teachers, Title I teachers, and tutors. There is a danger of making instruction fragmented, with teachers using their own favorite materials or sequence of skills when working with children. Administrators must coordinate the efforts of all these individuals to insure that the children are not being pulled in different directions.

What is the Administrator's Role in Relation to Parents?

Administrators are key persons between staff and parents. The administrator is most often the first person to interpret the reading program to parents enrolling children in a new school. It is therefore important that administrators understand goals and objectives. As children mirror their parents, schools often mirror their leaders. A

Olson, Childs, and Hammond

school, then, is a direct result of the interaction of that staff and administrator.

Successful administrators must be able to relate to people. Communication is a key concept. Administrators are constantly communicating—listening as well as speaking—with children, staff, colleagues, curriculum leaders, parents, and the community.

It is helpful to schedule fall meetings for parents. At this time the school curriculum can be explained. The administrator, reading specialist, and/or staff can explain the goals of the reading program, the record-keeping system used, and how the building is organized for reading. Communication cannot stop there but must continue throughout the year. Monthly notes indicating each child's progress within the reading program are eminently helpful. Conferences afford an opportunity for the parents to seek answers to questions about their child's 1) attitude toward reading readiness, 2) progress in learning the alphabet, 3) progress in related skills (visual discrimination, auditory discrimination, left-to-right orientation printing), 4) class group and general progress with respect to grade level, 5) expectations for first grade follow up, and 6) need for review or enrichment at home.

What Guildelines Will the Administrator Need?

The administrator is subject to any directives or guidelines given by the superintendent, curriculum director, or elementary director. For example, there may be a district reading policy of "ceilings off"— meaning a second grade child can read in material beyond second grade level. There may also be district requirements on testing, mastery of skills, or record-keeping. It is the responsibility of the administrator to enforce these guidelines established by the district.

Administrators may include guidelines of their own concerning lesson plans, maximum number of children within a reading group, number of reading groups per room, or provision of adequate time for teaching reading.

Summary

Administrators have a key role in any beginning reading program. First, they must understand and appreciate the existence of individual differences among kindergarten children. Once this premise is accepted, the administrator and kindergarten teachers go about the task of developing each child's abilities.

Second, administrators need to realize the increasing curricular demands made on kindergarten teachers, while the time for instruction remains the same. It is important for the administrator to become involved in decisions about curriculum priorities. In addition to curricular concerns, the administrator needs to promote professional cooperation among kindergarten teachers as well as among the entire staff. One highly important goal is to develop staff cohesiveness.

A third consideration has to do with the use of personnel and financial resources. For any beginning reading program to be successful, funding must be available for necessary materials. Supplying a kindergarten room is considerably different and often more expensive than for other grades. Also, it is important that kindergarten classes receive equal time from all support personnel.

A fourth role for administrators is one of leadership and supervision of the reading program. The administrator does not need to be an expert in reading but should use sound practices of administration and supervision and seek the assistance of the building reading specialist or district reading consultant on matters of sound reading instruction. Effective supervision requires regular classroom observations.

Finally, administrators must be able to relate well to many people as they communicate with the children, staff, colleagues, curriculum leaders, parents, and community.

References

1. Harris, L.A., and C.B. Smith. *Reading Instruction through Diagnostic Teaching.* New York: Holt, Rinehart, and Winston, 1972.
2. Singer, Harry. "Resolving Curricular Conflicts in the 1970s: Modifying the Hypothesis, It's the Teacher Who Makes the Difference in Reading Achievement," Language Arts, 54 (February 1977), 158-163.

Planning for a Prereading Program 4

Joanne R. Nurss
Kathleen Telepak

The elementary school administrator is responsible for planning, implementing, and evaluating the school reading/language arts curriculum, including the kindergarten prereading program. All too often most of the attention is given to implementing and/or evaluating the program with planning being neglected. This chapter looks at the planning process and considers the steps to be taken in planning a kindergarten prereading program. If the prereading program is to be implemented in prekindergarten or first grade, the planning process is similar, although the content may be somewhat different.

The Planning Process

The first step in planning a prereading program is to state the philosophy and goals of the program. All those to be involved in the program, including kindergarten and first grade teachers and parents, should participate in the process. After the program goals have been established, two surveys should be made. The first is a survey of the target population to determine generally the children's backgrounds, experiences, and needs. The second survey should examine existing programs and resources. Based upon the information obtained from these surveys, the administrators, teachers, and parents are in a position to determine what type of prereading program is appropriate for the school's kindergarten.

The next steps are to assess each child's development in language and reading, to set specific objectives for each child, and to select appropriate instructional resources to accomplish those objectives. These resources include materials, methods, and personnel. The implementation and evaluation of the prereading program are discussed in chapters five and six.

Philosophy and Goals

The philosophy of any reading program should be that every child is ready for some kind of instruction in reading. Operating within this philosophy, the first goal of a prereading or developmental reading program is to enhance achievement in reading by matching the prereading/beginning reading tasks to the child's abilities and capacities. Determining the specific type of instruction for which a child is ready is the task of the instructional team. The skills of young children in such a program may range from readers to nonspeakers of English. To accomplish a match between each child's skills and the reading process, an assessment of each child is crucial. Assessment techniques discussed in chapter six should be helpful in achieving this goal.

The second goal of the prereading program is to insure continuity between the kindergarten and the primary reading programs. Knowledge of the instructional approaches used in the primary grades should aid in developing the prereading program. This statement does not mean the skills taught in first grade should be moved downward to the kindergarten. Instead, the kindergarten program should focus on developing the child's present skills and interests in reading, language, and related areas. For many children, the program goals will be to help them develop further their oral language skills; become familiar with books, stories, and print; and develop an interest in and reason for learning to read. For other children, the goals will be to build the prerequisite perceptual and cognitive skills necessary for success in the first grade program; to begin to recognize words and letters; and to dictate brief stories about their pictures or experiences. For still other children, the program goals will be expanded to reinforce their beginning reading skills by encouraging them to read books, to learn new strategies in word analysis, and to write stories. These latter goals are usually considered primary grade reading goals and are appropriate only for those children who have developed to that level of reading/language skill. Therefore, the kindergarten prereading program goals are to begin with the child's present level of development in language and reading and to move as far as that child is able, while remembering that some children are just becoming cognitively aware of the reading process while others are beginning to read or are reading fluently.

Survey of the Population

A survey should be made of the community, kindergarten population, and parents. A general description of the community served by the school should include such factors as 1) educational level of the adults; 2) socioeconomic level of the families; 3) language(s) spoken in most homes; and 4) academic achievement (particularly in reading) of children currently in elementary, middle and secondary schools in the community. The checklist given in Figure 1 will help organize these data about a community and its population.

Figure 1.   Checklist of Population

I. Community Description
  A. Name of community _____
    Name of school _____

  B. Type of area (check one)
    rural _____   suburban _____
    urban _____   small town _____

  C. Educational level of adults[1] (give approximate percentage at each label)
    less than high school _____
    high school or equivalent _____
    some college _____
    college graduate _____
    graduate and/or professional degree _____

  D. Socioeconomic level of community[1] (give approximate percentage in each)
    upper _____   lower middle _____
    upper middle _____   lower _____

  E. Predominant language(s) spoken in community (list)
    1. _____   3. _____
    2. _____   4. _____

  F. Academic achievement of school population

Grade	Date	Test (Name/Form/Level)	Subtest	Average[2] Score
_____	_____	_____	_____	_____
_____	_____	_____	_____	_____
_____	_____	_____	_____	_____
_____	_____	_____	_____	_____
_____	_____	_____	_____	_____
_____	_____	_____	_____	_____

II. Population—current and future
  A. Current kindergarten population (give approximate number in each)[3]
    children within kindergarten age _____
    children attending public school kindergarten _____
    children attending private kindergarten _____
    children not attending school _____
  B. Prior school experience (prior to kindergarten attendance)[4]
    children who attended private nursery school _____

---

[1] Data available from census tracts, school system office, or state/regional planning commission.

[2] Indicate type of score (e.g., standard score, percentile rank, or grade equivalent).

[3] Obtain data from a questionnaire sent to current kindergarten families.

[4] Obtain data by visiting programs or contacting teachers.

children who attended day care centers _____
children who attended Head Start program _____
children with no prior school experience _____
C. Type of prereading program used (describe briefly)[5]
kindergarten _____

_____

prekindergarten _____

_____

D. Projected kindergarten population (give approximate number projected for each of the next five years)[6]

19 ___ _____   19 ___ _____
19 ___ _____   19 ___ _____
19 ___ _____

III. Parents

A. Briefly describe the parents' interest in reading. _____

_____

_____

B. Briefly describe the parents' expectations for a kindergarten prereading program.

_____

_____

_____

---

[5] Data available from state/regional planning commission.
[6] Obtain from a meeting with parents or from a questionnaire.

If the educational and socioeconomic levels are high (for example, postsecondary and college education), one can expect the community to be interested in the children's educational success and to be able to assist the program in a variety of ways at home and in school. If the educational level is lower (high school education or less), one can expect the same level of interest; but there may be fewer community resources for direct assistance in the prereading program. However, a word of caution is in order. Many tasks that are needed in the prereading program can be done by persons who read very little themselves or who work during school hours. For example, such persons might laminate games with clear contact paper. Others might collect magazine pictures or cardboard boxes for word banks.

The community language background is important in order to know the language(s) the children will speak when they enter school and the language(s) most used in printed matter in the community (on billboards, in stores, in newspapers, magazines, books, and on packages and cans found in the home). If the predominant language of the community is different from that of the school (most likely English), a basic decision must be made about the prereading and beginning reading programs: Will the initial oral instruction be in the children's native language or in English (the school language)? Other questions to be answered include the following: How many children will be bilingual? How many will speak no English? Are bilingual early childhood teachers available?

A kindergarten prereading program may be under consideration because previous children in the school have had difficulties in learning to read or have made limited progress in reading in the primary grades. If so, the survey should include the reading achievement levels for the school population, particularly readiness test data at the beginning of first grade and reading test data at the end of first grade. These data suggest areas of skill development that might be included in the prereading program.

Administrators, parents, and teachers planning a prereading program also need descriptions of the current and/or potential kindergarten population. How many children of appropriate school age will be available? Are they currently in other private schools or day care centers? What are the enrollment projections for the next few years? How many children will have had prior nursery school or day care experience? What type of academic/language development program was provided in this previous school experience? Ideally, data about these programs in previous school situations will be obtained by visiting those schools and interviewing the teachers. If this approach is not possible, phone calls and questionnaires might be used.

Another major question to be explored is the parents' attitudes toward and interests in a prereading program. Is this something they support? If so, do they expect all children to be reading before first grade? If not, are they afraid the children will spend all day "doing workbooks"? The expectations of the parents are a most important variable in the success of such a program. If they are interested and supportive, the program is much more likely to succeed. Therefore, they should have significant input into the planning, implementation, and evaluation of the prereading program.

Survey of Current Programs and Resources

Because one of the aims of the prereading program is to provide a congruent program, a review of the primary reading program should be the next consideration. This survey should provide information concerning approaches and methods frequently used in the developmental reading program. Points in question are as follows: First, what approach to reading is used; i.e., linguistic, basal reader, language experience? Second, is the major emphasis of the approach a meaning (analytic) or code (synthetic) emphasis? Third, how are the skills sequenced; i.e., are consonants introduced before vowels?

The second thing to consider is surveying the resources for the staff. What inservice and/or preservice programs are already part of the school program? Would these training programs be beneficial to the teachers, paraprofessionals, and parent volunteers in the prereading program?

The third consideration in developing a prereading program is a survey of the materials already in the school. A plethora of materials in the school can be used in the program. Such items as books, workbooks, tests, or games may be adaptable to a prereading program.

A survey of the available school resources should be the fourth consideration. What resources, currently in the school, are applicable to a prereading program? Is there a media center? Is the center open to teachers, pupils, and parents? Are there books and records in the center for the beginning reader? What additional equipment from the media center can be utilized in the program? Many of the resources available in the school should aid in equipping a prereading program.

The fifth resource to be considered is additional personnel already in the school. These staff members, including the speech therapist, reading specialist, specific learning disabilities teacher, and teacher of the gifted, can be used to help plan and implement the prereading program. The school psychometrist, nurse, and social worker may also be able to give assistance.

The checklist of reading approaches and school resources given in Figure 2 may be beneficial in surveying the current program and school resources.

Figure 2. Checklist of School Resources

I. Survey of Developmental Reading Program

A. Type of Reading Program Used (check appropriate column)

	Frequently	Seldom	Never
Basal Reader	_____	_____	_____
Language Experience	_____	_____	_____
Individualized	_____	_____	_____
Linguistic	_____	_____	_____
Programmed Instruction	_____	_____	_____
Modified Alphabet	_____	_____	_____
Eclectic	_____	_____	_____

B. Method of Instruction (check one)
  Code emphasis _____
  Meaning emphasis _____

Nurss and Telepak

II. Survey of School Resources
   A. Reading Materials (list those applicable to prereading program)
      Basal Texts _____

      Workbooks _____

      Supplementary Books _____

      Trade Books _____

      Classroom Libraries _____

      Tests _____

      Reading Games _____

      Reading Kits _____

      Bilingual Materials _____

      Machines (i.e., Language Master) _____

   B. Language Materials
      Kits _____

      Games _____

      Tests _____

   C. Resources in the Media Center
      1. Materials (software, approximate number of each)

         Books for prereaders _____
         Books with records _____
         Books with tapes _____
         Films _____
         Filmstrips _____
         Science kits _____
         Maps and globes _____

      2. Equipment (hardware, approximate number of each)

         Record players _____
         Filmstrip projectors _____
         Film (movie) projectors _____
         Tape recorders _____
         Listening centers _____

D. Additional School Personnel (check those in school part- or full-time)
Reading Specialist _____
Speech Therapist _____
Behavior Disorders Teacher _____
Specific Learning Disabilities Teacher _____
Teacher of the Gifted _____
School Psychometrist _____
School Psychologist _____
School Nurse _____
Social Worker _____
Media Specialist and/or Librarian _____
Parent Volunteers _____
E. Physical Space (check if avialable)
1. General
Room for kindergarten _____
Furnishings for kindergarten _____
Basic equipment for kindergarten program _____
Outdoor play area _____
Indoor play area _____
Toilets, sinks, drinking fountains _____
Work area for parents _____
2. Reading Program
Quiet corner for library _____
Pillows, carpet squares, stools _____
Shelves _____
Instructional area _____
Table _____
Chairs _____
Chalkboard or chart stand _____
F. Budget (check if funds are available)
1. Personnel _____
2. Space (including utilities and maintenance) _____
3. Capital expenditures, if necessary _____
4. Instructional equipment _____
5. Instructional materials _____
6. Assessment materials _____
7. Inservice program _____
8. Parent involvement program _____

The Prereading Program

The administrator and other participants in the planning process are now in a position to review the program goals and survey data to determine if a kindergarten prereading program is appropriate. If the decision is to go ahead with planning such a program, the next step is to assess each child's current level of development.

Assessment of Prereading Skills

The major purpose of assessing prereading skills is to ascertain the child's level of development in each skill area in relation to the plans for teaching. Assessment by itself is of little value. Assessment of the child for instruction is essential. The purpose of assessment is to answer questions about readiness: Ready for what level of instruction? How will it be taught? By whom? With what kinds of materials? The administrator's major function in assessment is to consult with the instructional personnel (teachers, curriculum specialists, and testing coordinators) in choosing or developing assessment instruments in order to assure that they will answer the instructional questions stated above.

Assessment of prereading skills generally falls into three major areas: perceptual skills, language skills, and reading interest and motivation. The perceptual skills necessary for success in beginning reading are those visual and auditory skills to be used in decoding. The language and reasoning skills generally assessed are those related to the comprehension or understanding of oral language. Assessment of interest in and motivation for reading is more difficult to accomplish. The usual method is through teacher and/or parent observation of the children and their interests in books, signs, words, letters, and story records or tapes. Prereading assessment is generally accomplished by use of norm-referenced and criterion-referenced tests, observation of the child following a structured checklist, use of instructional tasks (mini-lessons), or some combination of these. Each of these is discussed in more detail in chapter six.

Setting Objectives for the Prereading Program

Setting objectives for the prereading program should be a cooperative process involving the existing school staff, the prereading staff, and the parents. During a planning phase, specific areas of performance such as building a sight vocabulary, increasing understanding of instructional language, or increasing listening comprehension skills, should be identified from the assessment data as specific needs. Using the general prereading program goals and prior assessment data as guides, the team generates a set of behaviorally-stated objectives which can be applied to individual children.

The objectives should be evaluated with respect to the 1) goals of the program, 2) available assessment data, 3) primary reading program, 4) nature of the student population, 5) financial constraints, and 6) instructional resources.

Examples of specific objectives for the prereading program follow. The children demonstrate:

1. An interest in books, in the printed word, and in reading through
   a. the choice of activities and materials they make during various activity periods;
   b. the questions asked about letters and words;
   c. attempts to write (copy) or read letters and words; and
   d. attention to stories when they are read aloud.
2. An awareness that reading is a form of communication by
   a. telling a story orally, seeing it written down, and hearing it read back;
   b. reading "rebus" directions for making something; and
   c. listening to information from a book to find the answer to a specific question.
3. An understanding of the directional nature of reading by
   a. looking at books from front to back while they are turned rightside up;
   b. pointing to or naming letters in a left-to-right direction and from the top to the bottom of the page; and
   c. beginning with the left page first.
4. A beginning reading vocabulary by
   a. correctly recognizing their names at sight;
   b. reading labels for objects around the room, both in connection with the object and in isolation;
   c. recognizing the names of other children in the class; and
   d. reading words used in connection with topics of interest or units of study, in language experience stories, and in titles given to art work, captions in books, and labels on pictures.
5. Increased speaking and listening vocabularies by
   a. using new and varied words in their oral expression; and
   b. demonstrating an understanding of these words when they are spoken or read to them.
6. An ability to understand stories read aloud by anticipating the next event, phrase, or word.
7. Knowledge of letters and sounds appropriate for the reading approach to be used (for example, an objective might be to produce the sound associated with the unstressed or short vowels and with a selected group of consonants giving the child the skills to begin building words composed of these letters and sounds; in another reading approach, however, the objective

Nurss and Telepak

might be to grasp that a group of words which the child now recognizes at sight all begin with the same letter, to name that letter, and to hear and produce the sound associated with it within the context of the known words).

After these objectives have been established, each child's assessment data are reviewed in light of the program goals and objectives. Specific instructional objectives will be set, methods and resources selected, and instruction begun. It is essential to a good prereading program that enough flexibility be allowed to adapt the program to the teacher's individual teaching style and to the developmental strengths of each child. For example, children whose assessment data indicates that they have well-developed auditory skills should be allowed to use those skills in the prereading program by learning the sounds and letters associated with them. Children with well-developed visual skills, on the other hand, should have the opportunity to learn words and phrases visually before beginning a phonics program. In other words, the specific objectives should take account of each child's strengths to assure success in the prereading/beginning reading program.

The process of planning, implementing, and evaluating a program is a continuous one. Children, materials, and objectives need to be evaluated in reference to children's skills, the prereading process, the goals of the program and the materials. Objectives and materials can be revised, as necessary, to match the children's skills and development.

Selecting Resources for the Prereading Program

Selection of the staff is most important because the prereading teacher is the central instructional component of the program. The teacher selected must have a knowledge of child development which can be readily applied to specific children, plus knowledge of the subject areas to be taught. A strong background in reading is beneficial and highly desirable in conceptualizing the child's total reading program. Knowledge of primary reading skills and materials helps the prereading teacher select resources to fit the child's present level of development as well as future needs.

Knowledge in these areas should be accompanied by some experience. Managing a classroom of twenty-five autonomous, initiating, and curious prereaders requires more than knowledge of their characteristics. Prior experiences with young children are important factors when organizing, implementing, and evaluating a program.

Planning a training program for the prereading personnel should focus on 1) understanding specific needs of the personnel and, thus, identifying the needed areas of training (child development, reading methods, assessment, or classroom organization and management) and 2) selecting the type of training program to be implemented (district-wide preservice workshop, a local school inservice program, or a college-based course).

Preservice and inservice training programs for the staff are probably already in operation at the school or school system level. The prereading staff may benefit from such existing programs. Inservice programs can encompass either on-the-job or off-the-job training. On-the-job training is conducted with a particular teacher or group of children and with specific materials. Training can focus on assessment techniques, achieving objectives, selecting alternative resources, or materials. Off-the-job training may consist of discussions, conferences, or workshops of special interest. Such workshops might center around teaching the bilingual child or managing a language experience approach in the classroom without a teacher aide.

Instructional approaches selected for the prereading program should reflect the goals and objectives of the program. If the goal is to integrate the child's language and prereading development, the instructional approach chosen (for example, a language experience approach) should incorporate books, films, writing activities, and field trips, all centering around one topic such as "The Farm."

Selection of books and activities to which children can relate should also be considered. Books about children, animals, or fairy tales are appropriate for children in Miami Beach, while a unit on "Snow" is not.

Figure 3 includes a list of materials which might be used in a prereading program. The materials selected for instructional purposes should be consistent with the approaches used in the first grade program. A language experience approach to prereading merges well with a basal reader program. This approach in a prereading program concentrates on building a sight vocabulary and later merges into phonic skills. When the materials and methods selected reflect the goals and objectives of the school reading/language arts program, continuity between the prereading and primary school reading programs is facilitated. If the primary program uses a meaning approach to reading, the prereading program should also use this approach. Failure to do so results in confusing the children and often delays their beginning reading. For example, if children have come to expect print to be meaningful and to communicate something, they would be confused by presentations of phonetically regular words grouped into nonsense phrases such as, "The rat sat on a fat mat." The children would have to "unlearn" what was grasped in the prereading program and learn a new approach to the printed page.

Figure 3. Materials Applicable for a Prereading Program

I. General Materials
   Paper, pencils, crayons
   Sentence strips, word cards
   Language experience charts
   Chalkboards (individual) and chalk
   Chartstand, paper, felt tipped pens
   Word cards and individual boxes
   Large pictures, old magazines, catalogs
   Lotto games
   Letto (Bingo with letters)
   Trade books (library books)
      Read aloud picture stories
      Information books
      Books with records or tapes
      Controlled vocabulary books
   Tape recorder and cassettes
   Record player and story records
   Filmstrip projector and filmstrips of books
   Language Master
   Flannel board and felt cutouts
   Magnetic board and letters
   Activities and equipment in room

II. Materials from Publishing Houses
   Reading kits
   Language kits
   Stories with tapes or records
   Trade books to accompany basal series
   Games, puzzles for sequencing, sorting, discrimination

Parents are the primary teachers of their young children and can, therefore, provide continuity between the home and school. Parents are interested and should be aided in working with their children at home. A beneficial parent training program would include topics on how to read a story, recommended books to be read aloud, how to use television at home, or how to teach reading in the kitchen.

Parents can be trained as volunteers to work in the school. Parent volunteers can become vital parts of the program because they have more time to spend with individual children. For example, if a language experience approach to beginning reading is used, the volunteers can write the individual experience stories as dictated to them by the children and the teacher can carry out the follow-up activities. Parent volunteers, if properly trained, can be instrumental in a successful prereading program.

Budgeting for the Prereading Program

The budget for the prereading program depends greatly on whether the school has an existing kindergarten program. If it does not, the budget must include teachers, teacher aides, inservice instruction, space (including utilities and maintenance), enclosed playground area, furniture, equipment, and instructional materials for all aspects of the program (art, music, movement, science, math, social studies, language arts, large and small muscle activity, and dramatic play). If, however, the kindergarten program already exists, the addition of a prereading program should add relatively little to the current costs. No additional personnel are needed although parents and/or older children may be sought as volunteer aides. Additional inservice training for the prereading staff can probably be provided within the existing kindergarten inservice budget. No additional space is needed although the room should be rearranged to provide two quiet corners—one for the library, equipped with books and pillows or carpet squares, and the other for individual or small group instruction, equipped with a table, chairs, and a chart stand or chalkboard. Additional instructional materials such as paper, pencils, word cards (with individual boxes for storage), games or the materials for making them, library books, individual letters to manipulate, and story records or tapes may be needed. The cost of these materials will be about $20 per child. Assessment materials will also be an additional item in the budget. Approximately $5 per child should be budgeted for assessment. It is hoped that an integral component of the prereading program will be a parent involvement/parent education program. Approximately $150 should be budgeted for communications, instruction (books, films, tapes, an occasional speaker), and refreshments. If no inservice program is available for the kindergarten teachers, approximately $200 should be budgeted for books, films, workshop leaders, and field trips. These budget figures are, of course, rough estimates and will vary depending on local costs, needs, and resources.

Allocating Space

If an existing kindergarten program is already housed in the school, no new space will be needed for the prereading program. If not, a large, cheerful room with running water, ample storage space, and individual places for the children's belongings is desirable. Also, an enclosed outdoor play area appropriately equipped and provision for large muscle activity indoors are necessary. The prereading program itself can take place almost anywhere, needing no specialized area other than the quiet areas mentioned.

Parents involved in the program could use a small work area off the main kindergarten room to work or meet in during regular school sessions, in addition to evenings and weekends. Such space, while desirable, is not absolutely essential. Parents should be involved in the classroom as much as possible.

Summary

Careful planning is essential to the successful development of a prereading program. The school administrator, in collaboration with the teachers and parents, needs to set the philosophy and goals for the program, survey the potential population to determine its extent and character, and survey the existing resources for implementing such a program. Once it has been decided to develop a kindergarten prereading program, the planning group must set the objectives for the program and assess the children's current level of skill development. Then the group must arrange appropriate instructional methods, materials, and staff to provide for the specific instructional objectives set for each child and to allow a smooth transition to the primary grade reading program. Administrators are cautioned once again against simply moving the existing first grade program and materials into the kindergarten. A well-planned prereading program for the kindergarten will take account of the unique organization of the kindergarten. Continuous planning, implementing, and evaluating by administrators, teachers, and parents will help ensure the success of the prereading program.

Organizing for Instruction:

Exploring Different Models
of Reading Instruction

5

**Terry Johnson
Margie Mayfield
Kerry Quorn**

There are hundreds of ways of teaching children to read. Aukerman identifies many in *Approaches to Beginning Reading* (3). Fortunately, there are very few models of reading instruction, and these models can be placed on a programed-organic continuum. At one end of the continuum are heavily structured, precisely preplanned programs that are carefully thought out, tested, and revised before they are acquired by the school and presented to children. An example of such a program is Sullivan's *Programmed Reading*. At the other end of the continuum are lightly structured programs that grow out of the interactions among the teacher, the children, and their immediate, current environments. An example of such a program is the language experience approach. Further examples are arranged along a continuum in Table 1. There are, of course, variations in the degree of structure among the programs listed within any one category.

Table 1. A Sampling of Reading Instructional Programs

Heavily Structured	Moderately Structured	Lightly Structured
Distar Reading Series	Bank Street Readers	Language Experience
Palo Alto Reading Program	Gateways to Reading	Organic Reading
Phonovisual Method	Treasure Series	Breakthrough to Literacy
Reading with Phonics	Holt Basic Reading System	Sounds of Language
Lift Off to Reading	Houghton Mifflin Readers	Readers
Programmed Reading	Macmillan Reading	Reading is Only the Tiger's
	Program	Tail
	Merrill Linguistic Reading	Individualized Reading
	Program	Language Experiences in
	New Open Highways	Reading
	Program	Instant Readers
	Reading 720	
	Reading Unlimited	
	Basic Reading	
	Open Court Basic Readers	

Heavily Structured Programs

Heavily structured programs such as the formal programed approaches with frames and immediate feedback have the advantage of insuring systematic coverage of the set of reading skills held to be important by a particular body of reading specialists. The frequent testings built into the program give the teacher the opportunity to consolidate student learnings before they progress any further into the program. One of the major disadvantages is that the focus of the programs is on skills rather than children. Such programs cannot take into account differences as learning styles and interests. The relative completeness of the program can be a two-edged sword. The expertise built into the program may make up for the shortcomings of weak or inexperienced teachers; however, such highly structured materials can rob teachers of professionalism if they come to believe that the program, rather than themselves, carries the sole burden of responsibility for teaching. Such an attitude can lead to teacher justification of clearly inappropriate activities for the children with whom they are working on the grounds that "It said to do it in the teacher's manual." A more insidious effect is an apparent loss of the ability to adapt the program should it become obvious that it is not working properly. This inability leads to program jumping which can become expensive: Program A is used and found to be lacking because, in the teacher's view, the program carries the prime responsibility for teaching; therefore, it must be faulty. Thus, there is a jump to Program B where the cycle is likely to repeat, leading to subsequent jumps to programs C, D, or E. Meanwhile, the expensive materials for the early programs lie unused and underused in a storage closet.

Another disadvantage of heavily structured programs is that the programatic nature of the approach requires that discrete items of language be isolated and sequentially presented. Thus the child may learn the sound /p/ and then /b/ and then /c/ and so on. As can be seen from Chapter Two, this is not the way children learn oral language and is almost certainly not the way they learn written language. Learning to read starts with a fuzzy (but unitary) concept of what to do and then is gradually brought into sharper and sharper focus as finer and finer discriminations are made. Programed approaches to reading tend to start at the wrong end (with fine discriminations), expecting the learner to learn backwards (from the particular to the whole).

Moderately Structured Programs

Moderately structured programs have the overall program preplanned with stories and exercises prearranged for presentation by the teacher. However, there is greater room for flexibility within this kind of approach than in the more heavily programed approaches.

Most basal readers fall into the moderately structured category (see Table 1).

The advantages of moderately structured approaches are the systematic coverage of skills and bountiful guidance, especially for the inexperienced teacher. However, this abundance of guidance can lead to the lack of initiative and originality discussed in the preceding section.

The greater flexibility of the semistructured programs can lead to greater precision in teaching if the material is put into the hands of a knowledgeable teacher. Particular reading experiences may have been incorporated by the program designers to achieve particular sets of teaching objectives which accomplished teachers who know their classes might well recognise as inappropriate for their students and, thus, use the material in a manner that is quite different from that suggested in the manual.

A great deal of rigidity remains in many of the moderately structured programs although there is considerable variety among these programs. Every basal reader by definition presents a body of reading experiences. These reading experiences are expressed in a particular style (or mixture of styles) of language and deal with selective views of the world. In a pluralistic society, it is impossible to present a series of readings that 1) use a pattern of language familiar to all children and 2) depict those aspects of reality that are familiar and meaningful to all children. Publishing companies have responded to the racism issue and are, at the time of writing, in the process of reacting to the sexism issue, but such modifications are often more satisfying to adult concerns than to childen. In any case, hundreds of minority groups are still stereotyped, underrepresented or not represented at all. Clearly it is quite impossible for any finite set of materials to encompass the changing nature of a diverse society. And even if it were possible, materials probably would not be sufficient. While a book might contain a story about a birthday party, the presentation of the story in the class may not coincide with the birthday of even one child. However adroit the program developers may be, their product may remain somewhat distant from the real lives of the children who are required to read the stories.

Lighlty Structured Programs

Lightly structured programs grow out of the daily events of the classroom. General teaching strategies may be planned in advance, but the actual content of each lesson and the language to express it will depend on what happens and what the children say about it.

The most serious disadvantage of such programs is the high level of expertise required of the teacher. In the hands of an inexperienced or incompetent teacher, such programs can become almost totally ineffective and possibly detrimental. The first children to suffer are the less able who rapidly become lost if adequate guidance is not provided. This disadvantage is most unfortunate since it is the less able children who often stand to gain much from a less structured program, such as the keyword or language experience approach. It is shown below that a language experience approach to beginning reading is an excellent way for young children to begin learning to read. Therefore, the demand for teaching expertise made by unstructured programs should suggest to administrators that, rather than reject such programs, every effort should be made to place the most experienced and competent teachers in the kindergarten classrooms.

Kindergarten children live in immediate and egocentric worlds. They bring to school highly idiosyncratic views and highly individualized ways of talking about their world. The lightly structured approaches to reading instruction utilize both of these characteristics. Instruction can be conducted on an individual or group basis. At the individual level the instructional material evolves from the child's own speech and thus 1) deals with what is of current interest to the child and 2) uses written language akin to the child's own oral language. Children witness the recreation of their oral language into written form. This experience goes a long way towards helping children develop the clear concept of the communication function of written language, discussed in Chapter Two.

Group instruction can dilute some of the benefits available from individual instruction, but the language used still has an immediacy as it is based on current events in or around the classroom. With the assistance of the group or class, the teacher creates a chart story around the care of the classroom pet, the newly finished group mural, a visit by the painters, or a proposed expedition to a local bakery.

In choosing an approach to beginning reading it is wise to consider the kind of language knowledge that the kindergarten child brings to school. As Chapter Two demonstrates, young children bring considerable facility in *using* language but have little knowledge *about* language.

A problem with many of the heavily structured and moderately structured approaches is that they require children to focus on, think about, and manipulate aspects of language which may be quite outside their current frame of reference. For example, phonics programs tend to focus on letters and speech sounds which may be based on concepts unfamiliar to the child. Whole word programs may require a child who is unfamiliar with the concepts of a word to remember the names of fifty or more words.

By way of contrast, lightly structured approaches such as language experience tend to focus on the use and meaning of the language rather than on the manner in which that meaning is expressed. This focus is one that is familiar to young children through their experiences with oral language. The parallelism between children's strategies in the learning and use of oral language, on one hand, and learning to read via a language experience approach, on the other hand, is a strong reason for considering its use in kindergarten classrooms.

The Place of Literature in the Reading Program

One important limitation of almost all approaches to beginning reading is an absence or dearth of literary language. Heavily structured approaches ignore it because they tend to be concerned centrally with sound-symbol relationships. Moderately structured approaches tend to focus on word control. Lightly structured approaches use *only* the language of the children and thus have a tendency to consolidate previous learning rather than lead towards control over more complex language, richer vocabulary, or artistic uses of language.

Bill Martin, Jr., in the *Sounds of Language* series and R.M. McCracken in *Reading Is Only the Tiger's Tail* show how these limitations may be overcome. In both these programs, it is suggested that the teacher present various pieces of recognized literature which are read and reread until they have become familiar. The children are then invited to substitute words and phrases within the frame of the piece of literature. In this way the children are introduced to an ever growing body of rich, beautiful language, are encouraged to make it their own, and then are invited to expand on it in a creative manner.

In any case, whether the foregoing expansion/substitution techniques are used, it is important that teachers incorporate a planned oral literature program in addition to the reading program. It cannot be too strongly stressed that the vast majority of instructional reading programs are not literature programs. Neither the inclusion of a few folk tales nor the occasional poem turns a reading program into a literature program.

The literature program is important for three reasons: 1) it is important in its own right because literature is an important and rewarding aspect of the world which aids in the growth of children's imaginations, 2) an oral language program is one of the best ways to develop children's abilities to listen, and 3) general language ability appears to grow through listening because as children encounter and become familiar with new language forms by ear, they are better able to cope with such language when it is encountered in print.

Johnson, Mayfield, and Quorn

Planning Alternative Grouping Procedures

While there are numerous reasons for grouping children, teachers have three basic arrangements at their disposal: individual, class, and group. Cross-age grouping may be seen as a variant somewhere between individual and group teaching. In planning various grouping procedures there is no necessity to view them competitively. It is not the case that one procedure is innately superior to any other; different purposes call for different grouping procedures. The goal is to use the arrangement that best suits the current need.

Individual

Individual teaching is an effective method of teaching reading skills because instruction can be modified in a way that is far beyond the flexibility possible in any other organizational arrangement. The difficulty is having adequate time to give to each learner. The successful implementation of an individualized teaching program depends on a careful mix of planning, materials, independence training, and room arrangement.

The first requirement is a commitment on the part of the teacher that individual teaching is a practical possibility. Fortunately, there has been a long tradition in preschool and kindergarten education of individualized instruction. Consequently, administrators may experience little resistance from kindergarten teachers to the idea of teaching on an individual basis. Planning for individualized instruction involves time tabling and materials selection. The teachers must perceive the necessity of planning for relatively long blocks of the school day when the majority of the children are working in an independent or semi-independent manner. It is during these times that the teacher will be working with individuals or small groups.

Acceptance of independent work periods carries with it strong implications for materials selection. It is necessary for the classroom to be liberally stocked with a wide variety of materials that the children have access to on a reasonably independent basis and can use without immediate and constant supervision. It is not necessary to limit one's thinking to reading-instruction materials when looking for such matter. Building blocks, water table, art supplies, play house, dress-up clothes, and a sand table are all devices that permit children to explore independently various aspects of the world. Appreciation of the fact that some children will be painting, at water play, or block building while others are receiving reading instruction must carry with it the recognition by teachers and administrators that there can be no block of time marked "reading readiness" or "reading instruction" on the kindergarten timetable. The teaching of reading may be going on all day with one group or another during many diverse activities (see suggested timetable in Chapter Three).

Selection of materials directly related to reading must meet not only the criterion of independent operation but also the need for an oral component mentioned in the previous section. An example of an apparatus that meets both these criteria is a cassette/book combination. The storyline from the book has been read aloud and electronically recorded on tape and stored in a cassette. The match between the text and the recording provides the necessary oral/visual association while the relative simplicity of operation of a cassette tape recorder means that most kindergarten children can learn how to operate the hardware and thus have independent access to the material. Electronic recording on a reel to reel tape, requires the intervention of an adult. Book/record combinations are usually less useful than cassettes for the same reason. Not all kindergarten children have the fine motor control to put on a disc recording, and often teachers are unwilling to permit them to try it. In any case, the wear and tear on records, phonographs, needles, and teachers can be considerable.

Card games or any material involving the matching of shapes, pictures, words, or colours are much more valuable if they have some form of self-checking built in. The presence of the self-checking feature increases the value of independent use of that material since the user can find out alone the correct answer. Observation of preschoolers using materials lacking such self-checking features indicates that often children spend more time waiting for the teacher to confirm the solution to the puzzle then they spend in arranging the pieces or the children repeatedly use the materials incorrectly.

There is little point in providing a wealth of material that children can use independently if the children 1) do not know how to use the material, 2) do not know where to find the material, or 3) feel constrained to ask the teacher's permission before selecting any material. It becomes necessary for teachers early in the year to teach the children where various materials are stored and in what condition they are to be returned. Rules must be set also as to when and how the children may exercise their own judgments as to what activities they will pursue. Teachers must also demonstrate how the various pieces of apparatus work and how they are to be treated. All this teaching may be summarized as independence training: the goal is that every child shall be familiar with the contents of the classroom and know how to function in it with some measure of self-direction.

Class Teaching

In the swing away from almost universal whole class teaching to alternatives, class teaching has come to have a bad name. However, class teaching has many advantages. In the first case it can be very efficient; if there is something that all the children need to know, it makes sense to tell them at the same time.

A more subtle but important value in class teaching is the sense of social cohesion that can be generated. Young children find routines reassuring and respond readily to such routines as the gathering together of the total group for news, birthday wishes, announcements or storytime. The last item, storytime, is particularly germane to the teaching of reading. The advantages of a regular storytime to a reading program are several. The contributions to both listening and literary appreciation made by oral reading by the teacher have already been discussed. Another important value of story reading is the modelling provided by the teacher. Many children come to school with little experience of being read to and may have an unclear idea as to what reading involves (see Chapter Two). Their confusion will be compounded if the teacher proceeds to try to teach them to read before their concepts of the function of reading have begun to crystalize. Reading aloud to children is one of the best ways of assisting children to develop this important concept. The children are presented with a daily model of an important adult (the teacher) doing this thing called reading. Being naturally imitative, it is likely that they will try to emulate the reading behavior of the teacher.

Another extremely important feature of story reading is the sense of pleasure associated with it. Storytime is one of the high points of the school day for many young children. If their initial contacts with books and stories in school are pleasurable, then it is more likely that they will approach the task of learning to read not with trepidation but with joyful anticipation.

Grouping

Grouping according to ability is a common organizational procedure. The somewhat rigid manner in which it is sometimes applied in the higher grades is inappropriate at the kindergarten level. That is, it may be inappropriate to have clearly defined, more or less permanent instructional groups with names and thinly disguised status differences. It is unnecessary for kindergarten children to know whether they are part of the "top" or "bottom" group or any other kind of group based on differences in achievement or ability.

A more appropriate procedure is for the teacher, having identified children who could benefit from some group instruction on a particular task, to call these children together by name and work with them while the rest of the class works independently or under the supervision of an aide. The composition of such groups can be reasonably fluid. If Drusila is engaged in a woodwork project when the reading group is in action, it should be all right for her to stay with her tools. Similarly, if Andrew wishes to bring his friend, Julie, with him to the reading group and she is agreeable, physical and cognitive room should be made for her.

While such tolerance should be permitted, the teacher should have a systematic plan. Teachers should be able to identify, for example, those children who are ready to make a start in reading, those capable of moving into printed material, and those who need more developmental activities before they can benefit from more formal instruction in reading. Furthermore, while allowing for day by day deviations, the teacher should ensure that over a course of a month, and certainly during the year, each child receives the kind of experiences that the teacher deems most beneficial.

It is evident that such a free flowing approach to grouping will work only with a relatively unstructured approach to reading. Selection of a structured reading program almost automatically locks one into a rigid grouping procedure. Suddenly children are perceived to fall behind and have to be pressured to catch up rather than being able to derive whatever benefit they can from the current instruction and thus progress at their own rates.

Cross-Age Grouping

Cross-age grouping (tutoring or a buddy system) is a variant of ability grouping in that both tutor and pupil must be picked and paired so as to maximize the benefit to both children. We believe it is a mistake to select older, competent readers to work with young children. We feel the older partner should be someone who is reading slightly below grade level.

There are three reasons for this belief. The first reason is that the older reader knows what it means to have difficulty in learning to read and thus is likely to be more sympathetic. The second reason is that the older reader needs a legitimate reason for reading simple material. Preparing to meet a young buddy will provide a respectable reason for doing so. And the third reason is that the failing reader is likely to be in need of some improvement in self-esteem. The special attention received in becoming a tutor and the superior status relative to the buddy will assist in developing a better self-image. To increase the likelihood of the acceptance of the older child's authority, the age difference between tutor and pupil should be two years or more. The parents of children selected as tutors should be informed and their cooperation sought. It should be made clear to them that their child is not being exploited nor used to lighten the burden of the teacher. Rather it should be stressed that their child has been selected for this program because it is felt that the benefits listed are likely to accrue as a result of involvement in it.

By the same token, the younger child should be selected with similar care. Children with severe learning or behaviour problems should probably be excluded. The most likely clients are those children who are experiencing marginal success and appear in need of sustained practice and application.

What actually happens between tutor and buddy depends a great deal on the reading program the younger child is receiving. However, tutors need careful preparation before and careful guidance during the program. Provision should be made for the tutors to meet together with the coordinator of the program regularly to discuss common concerns and to suggest future directions. The following is a partial list of activities that might be pursued:

Listen to younger child read

Read to younger child

Engage in echoic reading

Take down a story at the younger child's dictation

Play a reading game

Practice sight vocabulary

Engage in reciprocal questioning

Every effort should be exerted to make participation in the program a special privilege. For this reason, it is suggested that 1) the program should be of limited duration (four to six weeks); 2) the amount of time the children are away from their regular classes should be strictly controlled and of limited duration (three or four 20-minute sessions per week); and 3) where possible, both children should move from their regular classrooms and meet on "neutral ground" (library, lunch room, spare classroom, or learning center).

In launching a tutoring program, a cooperative approach is likely to be more successful than one that is imposed. A personal approach by the principal to a teacher of the younger children would probably work best. Teachers of older children might then be asked for their assistance. The program should be run through an entire sequence before other teacher pairs are formed. If the pilot program is deemed successful, involvement might be broadened. One individual should be designated as program coordinator and it should be made clear to the teaching staff that that person has the confidence and backing of the school administration.

The Classroom Reading Environment

Research shows that children as young as three are aware of the printed symbols in their environment (1, 8, 24). Educators (24, 6, 13) suggest that the environment does play an important role in the learning-to-read process. If this environment is a rich and rewarding one, learning to read is a more successful and valuable task. As Goodman and Goodman (13:13) state, "When printed language is part of that world, children will use that aspect of the environment if it is functional and significant to their life and culture." It is the responsibility of educators to see that the classroom environment is truly functional and significant.

The entire classroom environment should reflect the value and use of reading. Many different areas can contain items to be read daily by the children, including labels on areas of the room and their possessions, captions on paintings, directions to specific locations, procedures for using equipment, stories written by individuals and the class, labels on storage areas to aid use and return of materials, instructional signs such as "Quiet, please" in the library area, experience charts, postcards sent by classmates on vacation, the alphabet, a calendar, a map of the school area, and a list of class rules or reminders.

The Classroom Library

A classroom library has many functions: it is a place in which to read, think, relax, and work; a place to explore or to find information; a less frightening and more friendly place than the school library. The classroom library should be a well-established and visually significant area of the classroom. It should be spacious, well-lighted, clean, comfortable, quiet, orderly, useful, well-organized, and easily accessible. Soft furnishings such as curtains, cushions, and carpets are preferable to institutional furniture. Shelves and furniture can be arranged so as to define the limits of the library area.

The selection of books and pictures for the classroom library should be governed by two criteria. The first and most important of these is that the contents of the class library reflect and support the on-going program. Meeting this criterion suggests that the contents of the library should be continually renewed. As the teacher moves the class onto new topics, so the contents of the library should reflect that change.

The second criterion concerns the interests and maturity of the children. Animal fantasies, personified machines, folk stories, nursery rhymes, ABC books, and stories depicting their age mates are all popular with young children. Because books should be displayed with front covers rather than spines outermost, the number of books in the classroom library will be somewhat limited, a fact which will aid young children in making choices. For these reasons, the contents of the library should be changed regularly. Teacher, librarian, and children should cooperate in book selection. For example, some children can take orders from classmates when it is their turn to choose books for the classroom library.

A classroom library, to be an effective part of the beginning reading program, must be readily and easily used by all the children. The children should be able to use the area throughout the school day and before and after school. To assign or schedule times for each child to use the area defeats the purpose of the classroom library and discourages children's uses of all libraries. A classroom library is often the first step to a lifelong habit of browsing wherever there are reading materials. Such habits may best be begun when young if they are to last a lifetime.

The Story Center

Another section of the classroom environment that is relevant to the beginning-to-read process is the story center. The story center can be used by the teacher(s) and children and also by a child or a group of children independently. The purpose of the story center is to provide a place and the materials for the writing and reading of children's stories.

In applying the general organization criteria, the story center must be a defined area with adequate lighting; it should also be attractive, accessible, well-organized, and appropriate to the children and the reading program.

Equipment and materials typically found in the story center include chairs and tables of appropriate size for young children, different types of paper (wide-lined, narrow-lined, newsprint, story-picture, index cards, chart paper), a variety of writing instruments (pencils of different sizes and colors, pens, felt tip markers, a typewriter, printing sets, crayons, chalk), dictionaries (both published and teacher and/or student-made), and key word cards. Other support equipment can include a chalkboard for writing stories with the entire class; a bulletin board for displaying the children's work; and a variety of pictures, posters, and objects to motivate discussion and writing. Many teachers also find a large, upright metal frame useful for displaying chart paper. The story center in a class of beginning readers, especially early in the year, might also include materials to stimulate language, such as puppets, flannel boards with felt pieces, magnetic boards, cassette recorders, and language masters.

Learning Centers

Another type of center found in many beginning reading classrooms is the learning center. Basically, a learning center is an instructional area developed for a specific goal (e.g., teaching beginning consonant sounds or practicing rhyming words). Learning centers often permit the best use of classroom space while fostering such skills and fulfilling such needs as independent learning, self-motivation, cooperation, individual differences, and efficient use of time, as well as providing variety and fun in learning.

In addition, learning centers should be well-planned, flexible, openended, durable, well-supervised, and as self-correcting as possible. There are many excellent books (see bibliography) which detail the steps in establishing learning centers and provide examples of learning centers in the primary classroom.

Other materials that should be included are manipulatives of various kinds: matching card games, name cards for labelling various objects around the room, simple jigsaw puzzles, magnetic pieces, and so forth. An important criterion for selection is that the basic units of the apparatus be simple and capable of being arranged and rearranged in many different ways. A box of wooden blocks meets this criterion very well. Elaborate mechanical or electrical toys which permit the child to serve only as a relatively passive observer have little educational benefit.

The actual classroom placement of the learning centers may be determined to some extent by the physical characteristics of the room. Provided the general and specific organization criteria are met, learning centers can be accommodated in many small nooks, corners, and crannies. Often otherwise dead space can be put to profitable use. Areas for learning centers can be created by thoughtful arrangements of cabinets, shelves, storage units, carrels, dividers, easels, bulletin boards, etc. Large appliance boxes can be adapted to provide the necessary furniture for a center. Tri-wall cardboard is another quick and inexpensive material for providing additional pieces of furniture. The lower half of a classroom closet or a cupboard also might be utilized. Some centers can be made portable to allow for varied choices in location.

Providing Continuity of the Program within the Building

While in the past, concern for the reading program has focused on the individual teacher in each classroom, there is growing evidence that the total reading program in the school needs to be the major concern. Singer (20) identified three exemplary reading programs. One of the major characteristics of these programs was that they were coordinated school or district programs. The best individual classroom program is a failure if it causes students to have problems in later grades.

As schools and districts consider the role of reading in the kindergarten, one of the concerns must be to ensure that the total program is coordinated so that teachers aren't working in isolation. The Denver studies of early reading (5) found that children could begin reading in kindergarten but any gains made were later lost unless the program was adjusted in the other grades as well.

One strategy that administrators can use to encourage program coordination in a school follows:

1. A definition of a competent reader is developed.
2. This definition is divided into a series of eight to ten goals of reading instruction for a child leaving the school at grade six.
3. The school staff discusses each of these goals and tries to assign responsibilities among themselves for reaching these goals.
4. Assigned responsibilities are adjusted as needed.

The purpose of the activity is to focus discussion on the children's achievements and to overcome reliance on commercially prepared reading programs as the final determiner of program direction.

Cross-grade meetings are a second way to encourage program coordination. These meetings are most needed at transition points in the school. For example, many elementary schools view kindergartens as separate from the primary grades and so meetings between kindergarten and grade one teachers are important. While there may be some resistance to these meetings (grade one teachers are more likely to meet with grade two teachers), they are essential for program coordination.

Cross-grade meetings should begin by emphasizing the common features of programs at the two levels. After people have discovered what they have in common, they are more likely to feel comfortable discussing differences. The first such meeting might focus on specific reading activities that are used in each classroom; later meetings could consider materials and points of view regarding reading or reading skills, while reserving for future meetings possible problems for children moving from one room to another.

It is not necessary for teachers to be in absolute agreement on the topics discussed; it is necessary that they understand and respect what colleagues are doing and also how they themselves can improve each child's chances for success in their own and other classrooms.

One of the concerns when developing a schoolwide program must be materials. The great majority of teachers use basal readers. Moving. grade one basal readers to the kindergarten classroom causes many problems. As is indicated in Chapter Two, an appropriate method for introducing reading to kindergarten age children is a language experience or integrated language approach (10). As the focus of a kindergarten language experience approach differs considerably from that of most basal series, it is essential that the kindergarten and grade one teachers discuss ways of helping children move from one approach to the other without confusion. The administrator needs to ensure that these meetings take place and to provide whatever assistance is needed for coordinating the programs. The particular materials chosen would seem to be secondary to the coordination of the classroom programs, the identification of possible problems, and the development of materials and methods to avoid these problems.

Summary

One of the major concerns when discussing reading in kindergarten is how such a program might be organized. When analyzing the continuum of heavily structured, moderately structured, and lightly structured programs, the programs that have been called lightly structured provide the best fit with the rapidly changing developmental pattern of kindergarten age children. Lightly structured programs allow the flexibility to enable children who are interested to begin reading and yet provide the necessary experiences to help other children determine what reading is. Lightly structured reading approaches require skilled teachers, however, so kindergarten assignments must be made carefully. Children's literature is neglected by most programs but is a necessary supplement for an effective program.

Whole class, small group, and individual grouping patterns should all be used when they are appropriate for particular activities. Flexibility and avoidance of derogatory labels need to be emphasized. In order to take advantage of the benefits of individual instruction, children need to be taught to work independently and the environment arranged to facilitate that independence. Clearly defined work areas with self-checking activities are the major means of facilitating independence.

The kindergarten program must be seen as an integral part of the school and district educational program in order to be successful.

References

1. Almy, Millie, C. "Young Children's Thinking and the Teaching of Reading," in Warren G. Cutts (Ed.), *Teaching Young Children to Read*. Washington, D.C.: U.S. Office of Education, 1964.
2. Ashton-Warner, Sylvia. *Teacher*. New York: Secker and Warburg, 1963.
3. Aukerman, Robert C. *Approaches to Beginning Reading*. New York: John Wiley and Sons, 1971.
4. Blance, Ellen, and Ann Cook. *The Monster Books*. Los Angeles: Bowmar, 1973.
5. Brzeinski, J.E., M.L. Harrison, and P. McKee. "Should Johnny Read in Kindergarten?" *National Education Association Journal*, 56 (1967), 23-25.
6. Davis, David, et al. *Playway: Education for Reality*. Minneapolis: Winston Press, 1973.
7. Downing, J.A. "Children's Concepts of Language in Learning to Read," *Educational Research*, 12 (1970) 106-112.
8. Durkin, Dolores. *Children Who Read Early: Two Longitudinal Studies*. New York: Teachers College Press, 1966.
9. Durkin, Dolores. *Strategies for Identifying Words*. Boston: Allyn and Bacon, 1976.
10. Durkin, Dolores. *Teaching Young Children to Read*. Boston: Allyn and Bacon, 1972.
11. Fitts, P.M., and M.I. Posner. *Human Performance*. Belmont, California: Brooks-Cole, 1967.

Johnson, Mayfield, and Quorn

12. Glass, Gerald. "The Teaching of Word Analysis through Perceptual Conditioning," in J.A. Figurel (Ed.), *Reading and Inquiry*. Newark, Delaware: International Reading Association, 1965.
13. Goodman, Kenneth S., and Yetta M. Goodman. "Learning to Read is Natural," paper presented at the Conference on Theory and Practice of Beginning Reading Instruction, Pittsburgh, April 13, 1976.
14. Hall, MaryAnne. *Teaching Reading as a Language Experience*. Columbus, Ohio: Charles E. Merrill, 1970.
15. Harris, Albert J., et al. (Eds.). *Macmillan Reading Program,* Revised Edition. Riverside, New Jersey: Macmillan, 1974.
16. Herber, Harold L. *Reading in the Content Areas*. Englewood Cliffs, New Jersey: Prentice-Hall, 1970.
17. Lee, Doris M., and Roach Van Allen. *Learning to Read through Experience*. New York: Appleton-Century-Crofts, 1963.
18. MacKay, D.M., B. Thompson, and P. Schaub. *Breakthrough to Literacy (Teacher's Manual): The Theory and Practice of Teaching Initial Reading and Writing*. London: Longmans for Schools Council, 1970.
19. Reid, J.F. "Learning to Think about Reading," *Reading,* 1 (1967), 56-62.
20. Singer, Harry. "Resolving Curricular Conflicts in the 1970s: Modifying the Hypothesis, It's the Teacher Who Makes the Difference in Reading Achievement," *Language Arts,* 54 (February 1977), 158-163.
21. Smith, Frank. "Learning to Read by Reading," *Language Arts,* 53 (1976), 297-299, 322.
22. Smith, Frank. *Understanding Reading*. New York: Holt, Rinehart and Winston, 1971.
23. Stauffer, R.G. *Directing the Reading-Thinking Process*. New York: Harper and Row, 1975.
24. Stauffer, Russell G. *The Language Experience Approach to the Teaching of Reading*. New York: Harper and Row, 1970.
25. Suid, Murray. "We Live In a World of Symbols," *Learning,* 1 (1972), 32-45.

Learning Centers

ASCD *Creating a Good Environment for Learning*. Washington, D.C.: ASCD, 1954.
Barratta-Lorton, Mary. *Work Jobs: Activity Centered Learning for Early Childhood Education*. Atlanta, Georgia: Addison-Wesley, 1972.
Danoff, Judith, et al. *Open for Children*. New York: McGraw-Hill, 1977.
Davidson, Tom, et al. *The Learning Center Book: An Integrated Approach*. Pacific Palisades, California: Goodyear Publishing, 1976.
Day, Barbara. *Open Learning in Early Childhood*. New York: Macmillan, 1975.
Flemming, Bonnie Mack, et al. *Resources for Creative Teaching in Early Childhood Education*. New York: Harcourt Brace Jovanovich, 1977.
Forte, Imagene, et al. *Center Stuff for Nooks, Crannies, and Corners*. Nashville: Incentive Publications, 1973.
Kaplan, Sandra N., et al. *Change for Children*. Pacific Palisades, California: Goodyear Publishing, 1973.
Nations, Jimmy E. (Ed.). *Learning Centers in the Classroom*. Washington, D.C.: NEA, 1976.
Rapport, Virginia, and Mary N.S.W. Parker. *Learning Centers: Children on Their Own*. Washington, D.C.: ACEI, 1970.
Voight, Ralph C. *Invitation to Learning: The Learning Center Handbook*. Washington, D.C.: Acropolis Books, 1971.

Reading Programs

Allen, R.V., and C. Allen. *Language Experiences in Reading*. Chicago: Encyclopedia Brittanica, 1966, 1967.

Ashton-Warner, Sylvia. *Teacher*. New York: Simon and Schuster, 1963.

Bank Street Readers, Revised Edition. Bank Street College of Education. Riverside, New Jersey: Macmillan, 1972, 1973.

Clymer, Theodore, et al. *Reading 720*. Lexington, Massachusetts: Ginn, 1976.

Durr, William K., et al. *Houghton Mifflin Readers*. Boston: Houghton Mifflin, 1974.

Engelmann, Siegfried, and Elaine C. Bruner. *Distar Reading Series*, Revised Edition. Chicago: Science Research Associates, 1969.

Evertts, E.L., et al. *Holt Basic Reading System*. New York: Holt, Rinehart and Winston, 1973.

Fries, Charles E., et al. *Merrill Linguistic Reading Program*. Columbus, Ohio: Charles E. Merrill Publishing, 1975.

Glim, Theodore E. *Palo Alto Reading Program: Sequential Steps in Reading*, Second Edition. New York: Harcourt Brace Jovanovich, 1973.

Hay, Julie, et al. *Reading with Phonics*. Philadelphia: J.B. Lippincott, 1967.

Johnson, I., et al. *New Open Highways Program*. Glenview, Illinois: Scott, Foresman, 1974.

Mackay, David, et al. *Breakthrough to Literacy Series*. Los Angeles: Bowmar, 1973.

Martin, Bill Jr., and Peggy Brogan. *Instant Readers*. New York: Holt, Rinehart and Winston, 1970.

Martin, Bill Jr., and Peggy Brogan. *Sounds of Language Readers*. New York: Holt, Rinehart and Winston, 1970.

McCracken, Robert, et al. *Reading Is Only the Tiger's Tail*. San Rafael, California: Leswing Press, 1972.

Open Court Basic Readers. La Salle, Illinois: Open Court, 1965.

Reading Unlimited, Revised Edition. Glenview, Illinois: Scott, Foresman Systems, 1976.

Schoolfield, Lucille D., et al. *The Phonovisual Method*. Washington, D.C.: Phonovisual Products, no date.

Shane, Harold G., and Kathleen B. Hester. *Gateways to Reading Teasures Series*. River Forest, Illinois: Laidlaw Brothers, no date.

Sullivan Associates. *Programmed Reading*. New York: McGraw-Hill.

Veatch, Jeannette. *Individualizing Your Reading Program*. New York: G.P. Putnam and Sons, 1959.

Woolman, Myron. *Lift-Off to Reading*. Chicago: Science Research Associates, 1966.

Continuous
Diagnosis and
Assessment 6 Edward Paradis

Responsibilities of the administrator to a beginning reading program have been the concern of earlier chapters: understanding of young children's growth, participation in the planning for the instructional program, assisting in organizing for instruction, and working with teachers and parents in the program. An additional responsibility of the administrator is an awareness of the evaluation procedure for the program. The evaluation is a twofold process beginning with the continuous diagnosis of children's growth in reading ability, cognitive development, and attitude toward reading. The second part of the evaluation is the continuous assessment of program objectives, teaching strategies, organization, and materials.

Continuous diagnosis is the evaluation throughout the year of individual children's growth in skills and subskills identified as a part of the reading process. In addition, diagnosis examines the cognitive development and growth in interest in reading. The diagnosis is most often conducted by the classroom teacher as it is closely related to daily instruction and most effectively done in the instructional setting.

Continuous assessment is the evaluation of the success of the overall beginning reading program. The assessment examines the appropriateness of program objectives, the effectiveness of teaching strategies, the efficiency of instructional organization, and the value of materials. Program assessment is normally conducted throughout the instructional year with a major emphasis placed on the evaluation of the entire program at the end of the year. The classroom teacher conducts the assessment of specific objectives throughout the year while the administrator has a more active role in the end of year evaluation.

Continuous diagnosis and continuous assessment are closely related as overlap occurs in the instructional setting. The results of diagnosis provide information as to which factors should be examined when assessing the program. If the diagnosis indicates that certain instructional objectives of the program are not attained, then the assessment should examine teaching strategies, organization, and materials to determine if they have been effective. If the strategies, organization, and materials are judged effective, the objectives should be reexamined to determine whether they are appropriate. A comprehensive evaluation should determine whether children are mastering the reading skills and subskills being taught; whether the teaching strategies, organization, and materials are effective; and whether the objectives being stressed are appropriate.

This chapter explores the processes of continuous diagnosis and assessment. Descriptions and procedures are presented and the roles of teacher and administrator are discussed.

Continuous Diagnosis of Children's Needs and Progress

Continuous diagnosis is an integral element in a beginning reading program as it provides for the evaluation of children's growth throughout the year. Information gained from the diagnosis may be used to adjust the level of instruction in order to increase the likelihood of success for each child. Providing maximum opportunities for success is crucial as feelings of failure are too often associated with a negative emotional reaction to reading instruction. Continuous diagnosis reduces the chances of repeated failure since the child is evaluated daily and adjustments can be made immediately.

Formal Measures

Continuous diagnosis should consider measures of both a formal and informal nature. Formal instruments include reading readiness tests such as the Metropolitan Readiness Test and language related tests such as the Illinois Test of Psycholinguistic Ability. These formal instruments provide normative data for comparative purposes and are considered to be objective measures.

Formal tests, however, have several limitations (8, 9, 16): 1) they may measure aspects of reading that are not a part of a school's program, or they may fail to measure aspects which are a part of the program; 2) they do not measure such important variables as attention span, cognitive learning style, and experiential background; and 3) they are normally administered once a year and, thus, are not of a continuing nature.

Informal Measures

Three informal measuring procedures are published tests, teacher developed checklists, and classroom observation. For continuous diagnosis, these procedures are considered more appropriate than formal measures as they have a close relationship to the instructional program and can be conducted throughout the year. The aspects of reading measured by the informal procedures are selected from the instructional objectives and examined in a natural teaching setting.

Published tests are the informal diagnostic procedures which provide the most objective measures. These tests are developed in a systematic fashion and usually include criteria for success but do not provide norms. Perhaps the most widely known tests are those based on behavioral objectives such as the *Wisconsin Design for Reading Skill Development* (20). Published tests have the advantage of being developed under expert guidance, field tested, and revised. The materials available from the publisher typically include a set of general guidelines, teacher's planning guides, resource files, and tests.

Published tests have also been developed by several basal reading series to accompany instructional materials. An example of these tests is contained in *Getting Ready to Read* (10). The individual skills and subskills are presented in a behavioral objective format and are keyed to the instructional materials.

A major limitation of published tests is the manner in which they are implemented. These tests can be used in a mechanistic fashion whereby tests are administered to all children at the same time, all subtests are given irrespective of the instructional objectives, and the results are recorded with minimal impact on daily instruction.

The proper use of published tests requires considerable attention. First, only those tests directly related to the instructional objectives are selected for administration. Second, children are measured on a frequent basis, and only those children who appear ready for the test are measured. Third, the results of the testing have immediate impact on instructional decisions.

Published tests, even when used appropriately, are subject to an additional caution. The test publishers typically do not provide data as to the reliability of the measures. The reliability of the tests may be low, posing questions as to what is actually being measured. When using published tests, teachers should continually examine the content validity of individual items to determine that the item does measure an aspect of instruction.

A second procedure for informal diagnosis is the use of checklists which provide descriptions of specific aspects of instruction. Checklists have been developed by basal reader publishers to be used with reading programs, and many school districts have developed lists. In addition, some checklists have been developed for specific purposes such as identifying learning disabled beginning readers (18).

The major difference between the use of published tests and checklists is the degree of formality involved in the measurement. Published tests provide a specific description of the item being measured and the precise criteria for measuring. Checklists provide a more general description and often do not provide recommendations for measuring. The teacher determines the criteria for measurement on checklists.

Allowing the teacher to determine the method for measuring can be either a strength or limitation of the checklists depending upon the background knowledge of the teacher. A teacher knowledgeable in reading instruction is a good judge for determining the method for measurement because the teacher is aware of instructional methods.

Determining method and criteria for measuring subskill attainment is best done by examining tasks from the instructional setting. If children are learning to discriminate letters and the instruction has been for children to find letters identical to a stimulus letter, then an appropriate method for measurement is to present a letter and have the child identify matching letters. Appropriate measuring methods are most often tasks similar to what the children have been doing in the instructional setting.

Checklists have a wide variety of appearances, but the content focuses on similar areas of competencies. Typical areas (12) included in a beginning reading checklist are

1. Auditory discrimination
2. Visual discrimination
3. Listening comprehension
4. Oral language development
5. General vocabulary
6. Relationship words
7. Sequencing
8. Following directions
9. Ability to categorize
10. Using oral context

Barbe (1) has developed checklists which could be used as models for the development of an individual classroom inventory. The value of Barbe's lists is that they provide a guide for items to be measured but allow the teacher to expand on specificity of the items and to determine the method for evaluation. Figure 1 presents a portion of the Barbe Reading Skills Checklist, Readiness Level.

Figure 1. Barbe Reading Skills Checklist, Readiness Level

(Last Name)	(First Name)	(Name of School)

(Age)	(Grade Placement)	(Name of Teacher)

I. Vocabulary
  A. Word Recognition
    1. Interested in words   _____
    2. Recognizes own name in print   _____

3. Knows names of letters   ————
4. Knows names of numbers   ————
5. Can match letters   ————
6. Can match numbers   ————
7. Can match capital and small letters   ————

B. Word Meaning
  1. Speaking vocabulary adequate to convey ideas   ————
  2. Associates pictures to words   ————
  3. Identifies new words by picture clues   ————

Teachers should be encouraged to develop checklists and inventories for the objectives taught in their classrooms. These lists may be more detailed and reflect specific objectives of the classroom. Checklists such as Barbe's or those from basal reading series may be used as references and models. Figure 2 is an example of a more detailed inventory developed from a portion of the list presented in Figure 1. This inventory demonstrates how a teacher could use the outline presented by Barbe to develop an expanded listing of skills directly related to the objectives of the classroom.

Figure 2. Inventory Developed from Figure 1

Name ———————————————— Date ————————————————

I. Vocabulary

	Seldom	Usually	Always
A. Word Recognition			
1. Interested in words			
a. Asks about words in the classroom	———	———	———
b. Recognizes labels in the classroom	———	———	———
c. Asks about words in books	———	———	———
2. Recognizes own name in print	———	———	———
3. Can name the following letters			
a. D	———	———	———
b. F	———	———	———
c. G	———	———	———
d. I	———	———	———
e. M	———	———	———
f. O	———	———	———

As teachers develop their own inventories, they should bear in mind that the aspects of reading being measured should be stated in terms that are observable and specific. The list in Figure 1 presents a broad description of items. Figure 2 presents a portion of the items defined in terms of more specific subskills and provides observable criteria for measurement.

Diagnosis and Assessment

The checklists discussed thus far have focused on skills and subskills presumably related to successful reading. A distinct danger of checklists is that instruction may be directed toward these lists and omit other important aspects. Braun (4) discussed the importance of children's awareness, during the early stages of instruction, that reading is communication. He cautions teachers to be alert to the tendency to establish sequential instruction toward isolated skill components that supposedly form the reading act. In order to maintain a realistic degree of instruction, teachers should also diagnose certain linguistic and cognitive aspects of reading. While no definitive list of these aspects exists, Figure 3 presents a sample checklist of criteria.

Figure 3. Sample Checklist for Selected Cognitive Aspects

Name _____ Date _____

Skill Area	Seldom	Usually	Always
1. Recognizes basic linguistic concepts			
a. Letters	_____	_____	_____
b. Words	_____	_____	_____
c. Sentences	_____	_____	_____
d. Numbers	_____	_____	_____
e. Sounds	_____	_____	_____
f. Spoken language can be divided into word and sounds	_____	_____	_____
g. Words can be built up from sounds	_____	_____	_____
2. Recognizes various purposes for listening to reading			
a. Reacting to the main theme of story	_____	_____	_____
b. Recalling selected facts and details	_____	_____	_____
c. Following sequence of story	_____	_____	_____
d. Predicting what may happen	_____	_____	_____
e. Expressing feelings of a character	_____	_____	_____
f. Recognizing real and unreal	_____	_____	_____

One of the most difficult tasks for teachers is the measurement of a child's interest in and attitude toward reading. The affective area is extremely difficult to measure objectively, but teachers should develop observable criteria to estimate the interests and attitudes of children. Figure 4 presents a sample checklist based upon affective categories reported by Koppenhaver (11).

Figure 4. Sample Checklist for Interest in Reading

Name _____ Date _____

Skill Area	Seldom	Usually	Always
1. Enjoys listening to stories being read	_____	_____	_____
2. Has a favorite story	_____	_____	_____
3. Looks at books during free time	_____	_____	_____
4. Discusses characters in story	_____	_____	_____
5. Acts out a character in a story	_____	_____	_____

Checklists have the advantage of being less formal than published tests and are more likely to be used on a continuing basis in close association with instruction. Children should be reevaluated frequently with a continuous diagnostic instrument, and the results of the evaluation should be used to assist in making instructional decisions.

The primary limitation of checklists is directly related to the major advantage regarding their informality. A checklist may be regarded as less important because it does not have the formal appearance of a readiness test or published test. This is a minor limitation when compared to benefits.

A third procedure for informal diagnosis is the use of classroom observation. Observational techniques may well provide diagnosis which is the most continuous as diagnosis occurs simultaneously with instruction. During instruction each child is observed by the teacher and diagnosed at that time.

The procedure for conducting observational diagnosis is to begin teaching the lesson, observe the contribution each child provides during instruction, diagnose each child based on the observation, and record the diagnosis. A source which provides detailed suggestions for observational diagnosis is *Teaching Young Children to Read* (6).

Two crucial steps in this type of diagnosis are observation of the child and record keeping. The observation should be a planned effort and considered an integral part of the lesson. Record keeping should be done in a systematic manner even though it must be recognized that it is a time consuming task. Checklists may well serve as the optimal technique for keeping records.

Observational diagnosis is difficult to accomplish because it requires substantial knowledge of the reading process and considerable time and effort. However, teachers should be aware of observational diagnosis techniques and encouraged to use them.

Summary of Continuing Diagnosis

An optimal evaluation provides an initial diagnosis or placement based on a readiness test or teacher judgment. Once instruction has begun, the most important diagnosis is that which is done by the teacher on a daily basis in the instructional setting. This diagnosis is less formal in appearance and accomplished by observing each child during instruction. The information should then be recorded on a checklist in order to preserve a record of reading growth. An important aspect is maintaining a longitudinal record which can be examined periodically in order to provide information for instructional adjustments.

Teachers should be aware of the need to measure cognitive development and interest in reading. Measurement in these areas is more difficult as criteria are less objective. Measurement, however, is crucial because the criteria focus on reading as an active communication process rather than a synthesis of isolated competencies.

Continuous Assessment of the Program

The second component of the evaluation process is continuous assessment to provide an examination of the success of the reading program throughout the teaching year. This assessment should examine the effectiveness of teaching strategies and the appropriateness of the instructional objectives. In addition, the organizational plan should be evaluated along with the instructional materials. Evaluation of this nature involves more of a subjective assessment than an empirical research examination (15). Measuring instruments of an objective nature are difficult to locate, and often less formal instruments must be developed by the local schools.

Bloom, Hastings, and Madaus (3) discuss three stages of assessment: 1) initial assessment, 2) formative evaluation, and 3) summative evaluation. Initial assessment is conducted prior to most instruction and incorporates the use of a placement or diagnostic test. In a beginning reading program a standardized readiness test or a procedure developed by the classroom teacher would most likely be used.

Formative Evaluation

The second stage of assessment is crucial as it is conducted throughout the year. This assessment is directly related to the objectives for each instructional task and occurs on a regular basis. Formative evaluation and continuous diagnosis as presented in the previous section are closely related as both occur immediately after instruction.

The relationship between diagnosis and assessment can be demonstrated by discussing a lesson for beginning reading children. Following instruction in a specific competency, the teacher diagnoses each child. The results of the diagnosis provide information as to the growth of each child and simultaneously provide an assessment of the instructional program as to whether the teaching strategies were effective and the objectives achieved. If the diagnosis indicates all children have learned the competency, then in terms of program assessment, it can be concluded that the strategies were effective and the objectives were achieved.

If the diagnosis indicates that the children did not learn the competency, then further examination is warranted. If all the children fail, the teacher should examine the effectiveness of the teaching strategy and the appropriateness of the objective. If the teaching strategy is judged effective, then further examination should be made for the appropriateness of the objective. When the teaching strategies are correct but children have not learned, the objective quite likely needs to be reexamined.

Continuous assessment of the program is, indeed, directly related to continuous diagnosis of children. The diagnosis occurs immediately after the instruction, and the assessment is based on the information from the diagnosis. The diagnosis examines the growth of each child while the assessment examines the program.

Summative Evaluation

At the end of the instructional year a second form of program assessment should occur which examines the objectives for the entire program, the organizational plan, and the instructional materials. Information for summative evaluation may be collected from tests, observations, questionnaires, and interviews. This evaluation is structured and conducted in a more formal manner than formative evaluation.

Summative evaluation may be viewed as having several stages. Rauch (15) presents the assessment of reading programs by recommending four steps: 1) clarifying the roles of the evaluators, 2) collecting the information, 3) analyzing the data, and 4) reporting the data.

The first step in a summative evaluation is to clarify the roles of the evaluators. The assessment procedure should gather information from many different people serving in various roles within education and the community. The evaluation team and the teacher should be aware that the program, not the teacher, is being evaluated. The teacher needs to have confidence in the evaluators if maximum information is to be gained.

The second step in summative evaluation is the collection of information for examining the program. This is a crucial step and should employ a variety of information gathering techniques. No single instrument should be used as a large number of cognitive and affective variables need to be measured (7, 15).

Possible sources of information include
1. Standardized test results
2. Checklists

3. Periodic observation
4. Questionnaires and interviews with parents
5. Questionnaires and interviews with teachers

The recommended sources have certain strengths in terms of what information can be gained, but each also has limitations. Using several techniques to gather information tends to minimize the limitations of any single approach.

A source of information often used is the standardized test which has the advantage of providing a degree of definitiveness (8). While these tests provide norms for comparison, the true composition of the reading process is unknown; and the actual relationship of the aspects measured by standardized tests to the reading process is equally unknown. Although the information shows how a child is succeeding in comparison to other children, there are portions of some readiness tests which measure aspects that may not be necessary for later reading success (10).

Another source of information is the checklist used for diagnosis and formative evaluation. This information is valuable because it is collected throughout the year during instruction and is closely related to the classroom objectives. The primary caution in the use of checklists is to be aware of their subjective nature. These instruments, however, often have more validity than standardized tests as the teacher developed measures should be more directly related to the objectives of the program.

To verify information from checklists periodic teacher observations in the classroom are used. Observations are usually more beneficial if some type of record is kept in order to provide a means of retaining the information. Figure 5 represents one type of easily used record format.

Figure 5. Record Format

Name _____ Date _____

    Instructional Area:

    Instructional Objective:

    Instructional Materials:

    Instructional Procedure:

    Comments:

Information about children's behavior outside the classroom may be gained through short questionnaires given to parents. Questionnaires not only provide information about the success of the program but also indicate to the parents the concern of the school for the child's growth in reading. Figure 6 presents a sample questionnaire.

Figure 6. Sample Questionnaire for Parents

Name _____ Date _____

The reading readiness program is currently being evaluated. In order to assist in this evaluation please respond to the following items:

	Seldom	Usually	Always
1. How often does your child look at books in your home?			
2. How often does your child ask you to read stories out loud?			
3. How often does your child bring books home?			
4. How often does your child visit the library?			
5. How often do you feel that the preparation your child is receiving in reading instruction is thorough?			

Please list additional comments or questions.
Thank you for your assistance.

The kindergarten teacher is perhaps the most knowledgeable single source for assessment information. A perceptive teacher-appraisal is necessary for a complete assessment of the program. The teacher-appraisal should determine the effectiveness of the materials, the nature of instruction, and the organization for instruction. Figures 7, 8, and 9 present sample checklists for each area. Items on the checklists were developed from information presented by Smith, Otto, and Hanson (19), and Brittain (5).

Figure 7. Sample Checklist for Examining the Effectiveness of Materials

Statement	Seldom	Usually	Always
1. Reading materials are consistent with philosophy and goals of the program			

2. Materials are adequate for various phases of
   the program
      a. Auditory discrimination
      b. Visual discrimination
      c. Listening comprehension
      d. Oral language development
      e. _____
      f. _____

3. The materials are
      a. Interesting and stimulating
      b. Easy for children to use
      c. Readily available
      d. Durable
      e. Well organized
      f. Cost effective

4. The materials accommodate the wide range of
   readiness abilities

5. I feel adequately prepared to use all materials
   available

Additional Comments:

_____

Figure 8. Sample Checklist for Examining Instruction

_____

Teacher _____ Date _____

Statement	Seldom	Usually	Always
1. A current record of daily activities is maintained.			
2. The daily activities reflect the program objectives.			
3. A record is kept of each child's current progress, instructional activities, and learning problems.			
4. An adequate amount of time is devoted to daily reading readiness instruction.			
5. Instructional decisions are consistent with other teachers working with these children.			
6. Students are progressing at a rate I expect.			
7. Current inservice plans are appropriate to my needs.			

Additional comments:

_____

Figure 9. A Sample Checklist for Evaluating Classroom Organization

_____

Teacher _____ Date _____

Statement	Seldom	Usually	Always
1. Pupils have sufficient opportunities for movement.	_____	_____	_____
2. The role of the student within the group is clearly defined.	_____	_____	_____
3. Student direction of learning situations is encouraged.	_____	_____	_____
4. A reasonable opportunity for success is ensured.	_____	_____	_____
5. Group stigmatization is avoided.	_____	_____	_____
6. Provisions for differing rates of learning are made.	_____	_____	_____
7. Flexibility of instructional time is maintained.	_____	_____	_____

8. Use of volunteers and aides
   a. Roles clearly defined
   b. Have the necessary skills to do what is asked.
	_____	_____	_____

Additional Comments:

These checklists should be viewed as examples of possible methods for evaluation. Teachers and administrators will likely find it necessary to adjust checklists for their personal use.

The data from standardized tests, checklists, observations, and questionnaires should be synthesized and organized in a manner useful to the teacher and the administrator. The analysis of the information gathered comprises the third step in summative evaluation. The following topics could be used for organizing the data:

1. Description of school and community
2. Objectives of program
3. Evaluation procedures
4. Strengths of program
5. Limitations of program
6. Recommendations

The final step in summative evaluation is reporting the data. The degree of formality utilized in the reporting depends upon the distribution of the final report. The report may be of a formal written nature if it is to be disseminated to the school administration and the community. Reports which are designed more for use by the teacher may be less formal and take the form of brief written comments or an oral discussion.

Summary

A comprehensive format for continuous assessment should incorporate several stages of evaluation. The initial assessment is important to determine the point at which instruction should begin for each child. Formative evaluation throughout the year is crucial as it provides daily information for making program adjustments on an immediate basis. This ongoing evaluation increases the likelihood that the program will fulfill the objectives as adjustments can be made early. Summative evaluation at the end of the year is important to the assessment of the entire program. At this time, children may be measured with more formal instruments and questionnaire type surveys may be used with parents and teachers. Using all three stages of evaluation, assessment is assured of being continuing and a maximum amount of information can be gathered.

Responsibilities for Continuous Diagnosis and Assessment

The primary responsibility for continuous diagnosis and assessment most often rests with the classroom teacher (2, 21). The teacher is with the children on a daily basis and the only one who can realistically provide diagnosis of a continuing nature. This diagnosis becomes the first step in program assessment and, if this assessment is to be continuous, the teacher appears to be the individual most involved.

The major role of the administrator is most often reported as being the instructional leader and providing motivation and encouragement (2, 13, 17). The degree of direct involvement is related to the extent of the administrator's background knowledge in reading instruction and the amount of time available for classroom involvement. Administrators must be selective in determining a realistic role for themselves in the evaluation of the beginning reading program. Responsibilities the administrator should consider include

1. Allocating time for teachers to develop measuring instruments and conduct evaluation.
2. Being familiar with the procedure used by the teacher for continuous diagnosis.
3. Being aware of the nature of formative evaluation used in the classroom.
4. Being actively involved in the organization, collection, and analysis of the summative evaluation at the end of the year.

Summary

Diagnosis and assessment are crucial elements in a beginning reading program. Children must be diagnosed continually to help ensure their success in reading instruction, and the program requires continuous assessment to determine if objectives are appropriate and instruction is effective.

Diagnostic procedures which may be used include 1) published tests, 2) teacher developed checklists, and 3) daily classroom observations. The most complete diagnosis incorporates a combination of these procedures.

Assessment of the program is closely related to the diagnosis of the children. Three stages of assessment provide maximum information for program examination. Initial evaluation provides for the placement of children for beginning instruction; formative evaluation provides a continuous flow of information throughout the instructional period; summative evaluation provides an examination of the entire program at its conclusion.

The administrator is the instructional leader for the beginning reading program and has a realistic responsibility for diagnosis and assessment. The major portion of the actual diagnosis and assessment should be conducted by the classroom teacher with the administrator providing the impetus thru motivation and encouragement. Perhaps the most important single element an administrator can provide is time to develop instruments to measure success and record progress.

The major focus of diagnosis and assessment has been on the aspect of continuous measurement. Collecting information throughout the year allows for instructional adjustments to be made early, a practice resulting in optimum success for the child.

References

1. Barbe, W.B. *Personalized Reading Instruction*. Englewood Cliffs, New Jersey: Prentice-Hall, 1967.
2. Barnard, Douglas P., and Robert Ward Hetzel. "The Principal's Role in Reading Instruction," *Reading Teacher*, 29 (January 1976), 386-388.
3. Bloom, Benjamin S., J. Thomas Hastings, and George F. Madaus. *Handbook on Formative and Summative Evaluation of Student Learning*. New York: McGraw-Hill, 1971.
4. Braun, Carl. "Diagnostic Teaching of Reading in a Language Experience Context," in Carl Braun and Victor Froese (Eds.), *An Experience Based Approach to Language and Reading*. Baltimore: University Park Press, 1977, 89-114.
5. Brittain, M.M. "Guidelines for Evaluating Classroom Organization for Teaching Reading," in W.H. MacGinitie (Ed.), *Assessment Problems in Reading*. Newark, Delaware: International Reading Association, 1973, 68-76.
6. Durkin, Dolores. *Teaching Young Children to Read*. Boston: Allyn and Bacon, 1976.
7. Farr, Roger. *Measurement and Evaluation of Reading*. New York: Harcourt Brace Jovanovich, 1970.
8. Farr, Roger, and N. Anastasiow. *Tests of Reading Readiness and Achievement: A Review and Evaluation*. Newark, Delaware: International Reading Association, 1969.
9. Harris, Larry A., and Carl B. Smith. *Reading Instruction*. New York: Holt, Rinehart and Winston, 1976.
10. Harrison, M. Lucile, et al. *Getting Ready to Read*. Boston: Houghton Mifflin, 1974.
11. Kopperhaver, A.H. "The Affective Domain: No Afterthought," in M.P. Douglass (Ed.), *Claremont Reading Conference, Fortieth Yearbook*. Claremont, California: Claremont Graduate School, 1976, 103-113.

12. Monteith, Mark K. "ERIC/RCS Report—Screening and Assessment Programs for Young Children: Reading Readiness and Learning Problems," *Language Arts*, 53 (November/December 1976), 920-924.
13. Rauch, Sidney J. "Administrators' Guidelines for More Effective Reading Programs," *Journal of Reading*, 17 (January 1974), 297-300.
14. Rauch, Sidney J. "A Checklist for the Evaluation of Reading Programs," *Reading Teacher*, 21 (March 1968), 519-522.
15. Rauch, Sidney J. "How to Evaluate a Reading Program," *Reading Teacher*, 24 (December 1970), 244-250.
16. Rude, Robert T. "Readiness Tests: Implications for Early Childhood Education," *Reading Teacher*, 26 (March 1973), 572-580.
17. Rutledge, Emma M. "What Principals Owe to Reading Teachers and Programs," *Reading Teacher*, 28 (May 1975), 748-749.
18. Sanacore, Joseph. "A Checklist for the Evaluation of Reading Readiness," *Elementary English*, 50 (September 1973), 858-870.
19. Smith, R.J., W. Otto, and L. Hansen. *The School Reading Program*. Boston: Houghton Mifflin, 1978.
20. *Wisconsin Design for Reading Skill Development*. Wisconsin Research and Development Center for Cognitive Learning. Minneapolis: National Computer Systems, 1970.
21. Zintz, Miles V. *The Reading Process*. Dubuque, Iowa: Wm. C. Brown Company, 1975.